Learning from Europe

Learning from Europe

Studies in Education Policy and Administration
for the AEC Trust

Councils and Education Press

Published for the AEC Trust by:
Longman Group Limited (Councils & Education Press)
6th Floor, Westgate House, The High, Harlow, Essex CM20 1NE, UK

© AEC Trust, 1984

First published 1984

British Library Cataloguing in Publication Data

Learning from Europe
1. School management and organization — Europe
2. Universities and colleges — Europe — Administration
I. Greig, Deborah
379.1'5'094   LB2900

ISBN 0 900313 19 6

Printed in Great Britain by
Butler and Tanner Ltd, Frome, Somerset

Contents

The AEC Trust

Trustees appointed on Charitable Incorporation were:

Chairman
Roland Edward Smith (re-elected 2.11.83) (Former President, AEC and Education Committee Chairman, London Borough of Redbridge)

The Rt. Hon. Edward Baron Boyle of Handsworth (retired 1.2.80) (Former Secretary of State for Education and Science and Vice-Chancellor, Leeds University)

John Race Godfrey Tomlinson, CBE (re-elected 24.11.82) (Director of Education, Cheshire. Former President, Society of Education Officers)

Leslie George Bowles, DL (re-elected 11.11.81) (Former President, AEC and Education Committee Chairman, Bedfordshire)

Richard John Laurence Jackson, CBE, DL, JP (retired 4.6.80) (Former President, AEC and Education Committee Chairman, North Riding of Yorkshire)

New Trustees appointed on retirement of former Trustees:

George Venables Cooke, CBE (appointed 1.2.80 and re-elected 11.11.81) (Former Chief Education Officer, Lincolnshire, President and General Secretary, Society of Education Officers)

Hugh Douty, CBE, DL (appointed 4.6.80 and re-elected 11.11.81) (Former President, AEC and Education Committee Chairman, Warwickshire)

Hon. Secretary
The Lord Alexander of Potterhill (Former Secretary, Association of Education Committees)

Foreword

When local government reorganisation took place in 1974 and the Association of Education Committees was compelled to discontinue, they established a Trust which became operative in 1978:

1. to meet their ongoing liabilities, and
2. to make such contribution as the resources allowed to the education service.

As a first step the Trust established a Fellowship enabling someone in the middle range of educational administration to spend three months visiting European countries to study a problem which would have relevance to our own education service.

Five AEC Trust Fellows have now completed their studies. This book sets out the reports from their study visits and endeavours to discuss the relevance of European experiences to current problems in our own education service. In each case the Fellows are expressing their own opinions of what they saw, and giving their own interpretations of what lessons may be drawn from their experiences. It is to be hoped that a careful study of the book will make a positive contribution to the education service.

Lord Alexander of Potterhill
Secretary

Roland Smith
Chairman

Association of Education Committees' Trust

Introduction

So much of value has emerged from the fellowships established by the Association of Education Committees' Trust that it was decided to make the insights gained from these studies of educational administration on the Continent more widely available. This book is the result. Five educational administrators have now completed their study tours: Derek Esp of Somerset, Clive McNeir of Northamptonshire, Michael Sweet of Solihull, Clayton Heycock of West Glamorgan, and Peter Purnell of Derby and South Derbyshire. They have reviewed and, where necessary, updated their findings for this book, and reflected on the lessons to be learned from their researches.

The impact of first impressions can be blunted by a return to the old routine. But, as these reports show, the stimulus that comes from seeing things done differently and often just as well - or better - can bring about a permanent change of attitude. Certainly the critical faculties are sharpened. With their studies behind them, the AEC Trust fellows can bring an outsider's perspective to bear on aspects of our own education system. They are prepared to challenge the *status quo* from the sound base of research into alternative practices. It would be an unwise commentator, Clive McNeir observes, who would venture to hold forth on vital questions like who should control the curriculum without having, as he puts it, 'the comforting knowledge that somewhere not too far away, there are people no less rational than ourselves doing things differently and managing them rather well.'

Since Derek Esp made his study visit to five Continental countries to look at the training and selection of senior staff in secondary schools, he has become an acknowledged authority on headteacher training, coordinating an OECD project internationally, and contributing to many courses and reports on the subject. The headteacher's role has become far more complex and stressful, he maintains. Nowhere is it clearly defined. And where its aims are implicit, they may often be pulling in different directions. 'We have simultaneously given the head more responsibilities and invented prescriptions which limit his scope for action', he complains.

In this kind of vacuum it is hard for headteacher training to flourish, Esp argues. We need to know more about what makes for *effective* headship if we are to provide training which will have a positive impact, he insists. How do we define 'effective', Esp asks. 'Do we want a chief education officer's "yes-man", a governor's door mat, or a teacher's pet?' What is needed, he believes, is someone with the skills and commitment to bring about school improvement.

Pointing out that some UK training schemes have had ambitious aims, but made little impact on our schools, Esp stresses that the aims and expected outcomes of training must be clearly spelled out. 'Too often conflicts of interests and perceptions have been left unresolved', he reports. One way to explore these conflicts is to encourage a far wider range of professionals to bring their skills to headteacher training. Esp urges heads, advisers, administrators, researchers and the teacher associations to work together here. And he does not stop there: 'Perhaps senior students in schools also have a role – in defining in their terms what makes for effective leadership and management in the school . . .'

The timing and siting of training are crucial factors, Esp maintains. He questions the value of training which takes place far removed from the school. Research in Canada suggests, he says, that it may be wiser to focus training on helping heads develop the skills they need to grapple with specific obstacles to progress in their own schools. Good timing can be crucial to success, Esp observes. 'Individuals and groups may be most responsive to training when they are about to face a new challenge or development in the school.'

Clive McNeir's analysis of the upheaval in the curriculum in the West German State of Hessen examines the fears associated with central control, and questions whether they are justified. From what he saw in Hessen, he is prepared to argue that central control may fairly be seen as a means of giving teachers support. It does not have to be identified with outside interference or indoctrination. He shows that for all the old chestnuts about classroom life in France or Germany, where every child will be poring over the same page of the same textbook at the same time, teachers in Germany have considerable freedom from control by examination board – a freedom many colleagues here might envy. In Hessen, the class teacher is heavily involved in setting and even marking papers for the *Abitur*. The traditional freedom of the teacher in this country may be illusory, McNeir suggests. The argument for autonomy may be used to defend a policy of non-interference which merely serves to camouflage a general unwillingness to give support where it is needed. Teachers here have far less guidance on curricular matters than their counterparts in West Germany, McNeir points out. 'I find it worrying', he says, 'that our teachers are so isolated when so much is expected of them.'

To leave teachers to get on with curriculum development may be hazardous at a time when the climate seems unfavourable to innovation, McNeir continues. 'It is doubtful', he feels, 'whether in these days of constraints on resources, heads and their staff will feel sufficiently free from threat to embark on bold curricular initiatives.' At the same time he is not convinced that the school, left to its own devices, can find all the answers to pupils' needs, or make the right decisions about finding room on the timetable for new subject areas like political education, conservation, and consumer education. These deserve consideration beyond the level of the individual school, he says.

McNeir understands why central control of the curriculum is viewed with a jaundiced eye in this country, but wonders if these fears are exaggerated. In West Germany, he says, 'it is recognised that a reasonable amount of political involvement in education is a further form of support, provided that the system has adequate checks and balances to prevent domination.' Teachers here who like to think their autonomy is guaranteed, should think again, McNeir warns. 'The days are gone', he says, 'when Secretaries of State did not presume to trespass in the "secret garden" where the teacher's responsibility was acknowledged as inviolate.'

Teachers have the choice of ignoring current moves to centralise control of the curriculum, or accepting that the curriculum needs a new stimulus and trying to get in on the act, McNeir argues. He favours a regional approach to curriculum development. But, whatever framework is proposed, he urges teachers to take account of the general unease about the lack of direction in the curriculum. 'Are we now moving towards a national policy introduced by the Secretary of State, or will we drift into a core curriculum based on those subjects which lend themselves most readily to examination?', he asks.

Michael Sweet's area of study – transition to adulthood – could hardly be more topical. One by one the countries of Western Europe have found themselves having to grapple with rising unemployment amongst the young. The measures they have introduced to cushion its effects are analysed in Sweet's report which also reflects on vocational work in schools and colleges, careers counselling, work experience, and preparation for leisure.

Adult education is extensively provided and well supported in the four countries he visited: Denmark, West Germany, Sweden and France. Though it may be a powerful force on the Continent, *éducation permanente* has yet to grow strong roots here, Sweet suggests. 'It is in the area of adult education that we are most deficient', he reports. 'The regeneration of adult education, both local authority and voluntary, is overdue, allied with a widening of its scope and purpose.' Calling for a review of alternative methods of funding for adult education, he says paid leave of absence for non-vocational adult programmes is worth considering, if early retirement and other devices for reducing the labour force are to attract support.

Experience in the four countries he studied illustrates the benefits of vesting responsibility for all young people up to 19 in the education service, whether they are in full-time education, on training courses, at work, or unemployed, Sweet says. He reveals that staying on rates in British schools are trailing behind those of our European neighbours. 'Staying on rates across Britain are variable', he notes. 'And there is a strong case for making education and training compulsory, either full-time or part-time, until 18.'

Contrasted with the well-established employer-based training he saw in Denmark and West Germany, and the education-based programmes available in Sweden and France, provision for the 16–19s in Britain bears all the marks of crisis planning, Sweet argues. 'We have been stampeded into policies and structures which could well fail the needs of young people in the longer term', he warns. What we have now, he argues, is a strange hybrid of further education, employer-based training, and programmes sponsored by the Manpower Services Commission. 'The mix is tricky and expensive to coordinate satisfactorily', Sweet maintains. 'Regional planning is complicated; there is a risk of duplication and waste of resources; and standards are hard to monitor and guarantee.'

The fact that for many young people there is no link between training and further qualifications is one of the major deficiencies of the Youth Training Scheme, Sweet says. Turning to the Technical and

Vocational Education Initiative, he questions the wisdom of investing £0.4 million a year in 250–1,000 pupils. He feels the same money could be used to better effect for a much larger group of young people of all abilities.

Schemes which offer subsidies to employers who take on extra labour have a built-in training component in the four countries studied. 'Without exception, our European neighbours recognise that merely rewarding firms for increasing their labour force serves only to disguise problems . . .', Sweet reports. He believes there is a great deal of scope here for imaginative subsidy schemes which would incorporate vocational training. He also feels we should consider a return to some form of national service. The issue is a sensitive one, he concedes. But he points to the experience of compulsory national service on the Continent and observes that one of its main objectives is to provide young people with training in practical and technical skills.

Clayton Heycock has looked at educational finance in Austria, Norway, Denmark and Italy. The different funding mechanisms he uncovered in these countries are ranged on a continuum from highly centralised funding to funding which is derived largely from local income tax. Heycock explains how they work, and draws from their experience the lesson that we should avoid the 'dangerous conclusion' that the only possible alternative for local government finance in England and Wales is some modification of existing funding patterns. 'It may be that radical thought is overdue', he says.

The early 1980s have been marked by intense financial difficulty in this country, Heycock says. 'It has been a period of difficult and somewhat antagonistic relationships between central and local government.' The signs are that things may deteriorate still further, he warns. Fears continue to mount that local accountability will be weakened by new financial systems as local authorities find themselves being saddled with more duties, but deprived of the powers needed to carry them out.

The overall level of local government spending has not shown a significant upward trend in the past few years, Heycock points out. Why then, he asks, is the Government so much preoccupied with the spending patterns of a few 'so-called high spending Councils'? It is wholly wrong-headed, he adds, to claim that our current economic ills are largely due to the spiralling expenditure of local government.

In the design of financial systems, simplicity and intelligibility are essential requirements, Heycock continues. 'It is vital that those involved in decision-taking are not confronted with a statistical mystique which defies understanding', he insists. Turning to the Grant Related Expenditure assessments introduced by the present Government, he says these are characterised by a degree of complexity which 'confounds most local government members and officers – not to mention the population at large'.

Reviewing the case for specific grants, Heycock points out that a specific grant is designed to provide monies for defined purposes: 'It removes a local authority's freedom to evaluate how to spend the money it receives.' He fears a switch to specific grants would result in local authorities being overwhelmed with detailed legislative and administrative guidelines, and is more inclined to favour the greater degree of residual freedom to be found in a block grant system which allows LEAs to distribute funds between different services. At the same time he argues in favour of local income tax, stressing that the maintenance of healthy local democracy depends on having a significant amount of funding raised locally.

Heycock is attracted by the assigned revenue approach he studied in Austria. It is relatively cheap and easy to use, he says. Central and local government work together to reach a consensus on which areas of taxation should fund central government services, and which should fund part of the services provided by local government. The approach has much to commend it, Heycock feels. Leaving funding mechanisms aside, he enters a plea for a longer financial planning period. 'It is not conducive to effective local government', he says, 'to have sudden changes in local government financial scenarios every few months.'

Peter Purnell's interest in multicultural education has developed since he moved from Dorset to Derby. Working in a city with a multi-ethnic population has brought home to him, he says, 'the need to educate all children to live in a society which is culturally diverse'. His studies in France, West Germany, the Netherlands, Belgium and Sweden have strengthened his conviction that governments need to show a clear-cut commitment to intercultural education if they wish to encourage positive attitudes among teachers, teacher trainers, education advisers and administrators.

Education systems in the five countries he visited have all had to learn to cater for growing numbers of children and young people coming from different cultures and speaking different languages. The children of immigrants now account for a quarter of all births in the industrialised countries of Western Europe, Purnell reveals. Schools are teaching more and more children who are second generation immigrants, born locally like indigenous children, but living in a different culture and usually speaking a different language at home. 'The educational achievement of many of these children gives cause for concern', Purnell reports. 'A disproportionate number have low levels of language proficiency and general attainment, often leading to placement in secondary schools with limited vocationally-based courses or in special education, and frequently ending in failure to obtain school leaving qualifications, and in unemployment.'

The decision in some countries to include intercultural education in initial training for all teachers, and to provide systematic in-service programmes for the teachers of foreign children, makes the situation in this country look 'patchy and uncoordinated', Purnell says. He urges the Department of Education and Science to give a clear lead to ensure that proper priority is given to multicultural education in teacher training.

Turning to mother tongue teaching, Purnell notes that although twelve per cent of British children from homes where English is not the first language are having mother-tongue teaching, only about two per cent of this teaching is provided in maintained schools. In France and the Netherlands about a third of foreign children are receiving tuition in their language and culture of origin, he reports. In Sweden, active bilingualism has been the major plank of education policy for minorities: two-thirds of eligible school-age children take up a right to be taught in their first language within normal schooling.

Purnell outlines the benefits to be derived from mother-tongue and bilingual teaching in schools. Their development in this country will depend, he says, on 'unequivocal official acceptance of the view that linguistic diversity is a national resource rather than a liability.' He calls on the DES to encourage local education authorities to increase their support for voluntary language classes, and find ways to coordinate the teaching they give with mainstream schooling.

Ethnic minority and foreign teachers should be brought into the education service at all levels, Purnell believes. 'Teachers who share with ethnic minority pupils the experience of more than one culture can', he argues, 'give considerable impetus to intercultural education – through their relationships with other staff and with pupils, and through their influence on the professional life of the school.'

Clearly, the AEC Trust fellowships have had an important impact on the professional lives of the five fellows and on the perspectives they bring to educational administration in this country. Other benefits are the new contacts and friendships they have made with professionals working in other European countries – links which are bound to serve the long term interests of the European educational community as a whole.

Deborah Greig
Editor

The AEC Trust Fellowship enabled me to follow up my interest in headteacher training. I felt then, and still feel, that the training needs of heads are not met adequately in England and Wales. An increasingly complex role, an increasingly turbulent environment for schools and the conflicting demands made on them, require a high standard of leadership and resilience of heads and senior staff in schools.

The AEC Trust Fellowship has led unexpectedly to an even greater involvement in this field. In my spare time I have taken part in an SEO review of training needs. I am also active in international endeavours to improve training provision. I addressed a Council of Europe research conference, initiated and helped to organise an international conference at Gatwick in March 1982 for nine European countries, and am coordinating that part of the OECD International School Improvement Project which is dealing with problems of "principal" training in fourteen countries. Currently I am part-based in London as one of the first two Education Officers seconded to the Audit Commission.

I am grateful to the AEC Trust for having this opportunity to extend my horizons. I cannot speak for their selection procedures, but I commend an AEC Trust Fellowship as an excellent in-service training exercise, and I thank the Trustees for the experience.

Derek Esp

Chapter 1

Headteacher Training and Selection

Derek Esp

Derek Esp, First Deputy Chief Education Officer with Somerset County Council, was the first AEC Trust fellow. He chose to examine the training and selection of headteachers and senior staff in secondary schools, and visited France, Denmark, Norway, Sweden and the Netherlands. His first brush with teaching was in the RAF Education Branch. This was followed by a short spell teaching in secondary schools and ten years in the youth service in Shropshire and Devon. Derek Esp moved into educational administration when he joined Somerset in 1969.

Comparative education studies present an author with many hazards, especially if the study is first in the field – or almost first. Perhaps the biggest hazard is that the work quickly achieves the status of an authoritative source document. With that accolade comes another problem – the author acquires instant recognition as an expert in the subject.

These hazards are greatest in the case of factual analyses – 'snapshots' of the state of the art at a particular date. This is why I would issue a government health warning with every report. In this instance what I described in five countries was the position in 1980. The situation has not greatly changed in some countries; in others the changes are substantial enough to modify the earlier impressions and conclusions.

In this 'revised version' I have interwoven later information into the 1980 report. I have added some thoughts on effective ways in which best practice and good ideas can be exchanged internationally. I have also separated out my original thoughts on 'lessons for the UK' and have attempted a longer analysis of the problems facing the trainers.

I made a ten-week study tour from January to June 1980, looking at the selection and training of headteachers and senior staff in Europe. I talked to Ministry of Education officials, trainers, trainees, teachers

1

and teachers' associations in the Netherlands, France, Sweden, Denmark and Norway.

The Association of Education Committees' Trust funded my visit and asked me for a short report of not less than 4,000 and not more than 5,000 words. With an allocation of 'a word a kilometre', this report could only be a prologue, and I went on to produce a detailed report on each country's training programme. These reports are now 'enshrined' in the files of the Educational Resources Information Center, Washington DC (ERIC).

My own restriction of the study to 'secondary' schools will require some clarification in the context of the countries visited. In Scandinavia it covered the compulsory 'all age' comprehensive schools (age range 7–16 years) and the upper secondary schools (16–19); in the Netherlands all general and technical secondary schools dealing with pupils aged 12 and over; and in France, the secondary schools with pupils over the age of 11 years.

Training in Europe

The training programmes I studied in each country were moulded by the structure of the education service, the organisation of pressure groups and, not least, the size and geographical features of the country.

There were two general assumptions behind the establishment of training courses for heads and senior staff. The first was that school leadership can no longer be exercised on the basis of experience and natural ability. The school leader needs to be trained in the skills of team leadership and the various pressures on heads arising from demands for participation, consultation and 'accountability' are well recognised. In the words of one French teacher: 'The head who was once on a pedestal, is now in the shooting gallery'. The second assumption was that the school (and not the head alone) should be given more freedom and autonomy to develop its own response to local needs and circumstances. This assumption prevailed, for example, in Sweden where 'devolution' is now a key part of organisational reform, and in France which presented the most centralised system.

In all five countries surveys by and pressures from headteachers have helped to establish the need for training, but very different circumstances have attended the introduction of training programmes. In France it was the events of 1968 that demonstrated the need for (and by 1970–71 the establishment of) a national training programme for teachers who were being thrown in at the deep end as heads. In Sweden the 'PLUS' Commission was established in 1972 to draw up a programme of school leader training.

About the same time the SIA Commission on the inner workings of the school began its work. This was a major commission set up to change the daily work methods of Swedish schools and strengthen relationships with their local communities. In 1976 two training programmes, one of them the school leader education programme, were established and funded for a ten-year period as an integral part of the SIA reforms. These reforms aimed to change the daily work methods of schools and develop their role in the community, giving many local opportunities for decision-making and spreading 'democratisation'. Swedish educational developments were very different from those in Norway and Denmark. Norway developed training courses on a regional or county basis through various initiatives by national councils for education, and Denmark was establishing a course for *folkeskole* heads in the autumn of 1980 as a result of pressure from heads who wanted something less 'academic' than courses provided in the past. In the Netherlands an enquiry by the headteachers' association and the interest of the then Minister of Education established the national training course at Arnhem in 1976.

The size and scope of the training programmes are impressive. The French compulsory training programme has provided since 1974 a three-month course in the April–June period for teachers who are taking up their first administrative appointment as head or deputy in the following September. Teachers going to all levels of management responsibility and all types of secondary schools are trained together. The course comprises residential sessions where main themes are developed, and periods of observation in schools, administrative agencies and private enterprise. The course provides a good grounding for teachers with little experience of school management. Short ten-day courses are provided for those with previous administrative experience and those designated as deputy heads in newly emerging comprehensive schools. In 1976 2,000 people were trained on the long and short courses. By 1980, following reorganisation, school mergers and the impact of falling rolls, 1,200 people had been trained.

The compulsory Swedish training programme provides for all school leaders (heads and deputies) from all types of school. Municipal school directors (chief education officers) and local politicians also take part. About 600 school leaders have been trained in each year since the courses began. To date some 400 of the 1,200 'headmaster districts' in

Sweden and half of the 4,500 school leaders have been trained. In the Netherlands, 1,770 people have attended the heavily over-subscribed course at Arnhem. Attendance at the course is voluntary, but the Ministry of Education pay all expenses. In 1979–80 a total of 550 heads and deputies from all types of secondary school and special schools attended the course. Norway has provided training for many years, e.g. 18 of the 19 Norwegian counties provide training for their upper secondary school heads, and training is generally available for heads of *grundskolen* (7–16 comprehensives). Other initiatives include a new course at Kristiansand at the Teacher Training College, which began in 1980. In Denmark, a course launched in 1980 aimed to provide 80 places a year for newly appointed heads of *folkeskoles*. Other courses in Denmark are provided by the headteachers' union and the main in-service training agency – the Royal Danish School of Educational Studies (*Danmarks Laerer Højskole*, or 'DLH'). A new course also began in 1980 for upper secondary school heads under the Ministry of Education's auspices.

In all the countries visited heads were eager to participate in training. In France, the Netherlands and Sweden a national training team is charged with the task of coordinating, developing and evaluating the training. In each case the trainers bring a wide variety of experience to bear. The Dutch team, based at Arnhem, also organises the courses. This approach is appropriate in the Netherlands, where the country is small geographically, and communications are good. In France and Sweden the central team of professional trainers provide a back-up service to regional teams. The 25 French regional teams (*équipes académiques de la vie scolaire*) of from twelve to 30 or so in size, are all volunteers, many of them serving heads who undertake the training role in addition to their normal duties. An *inspecteur d'académie* is formally given the task of coordinating the work of the '*équipe*'. In some cases a deputy *inspecteur d'académie* is given this task, and the time to do it, as part of his normal job. In Sweden the teams are led by a full-time trainer. His team members, many of them teachers, county inspectors and educational psychologists, are on part-time secondment. In Sweden and the Netherlands the national team have steering committees which enable the various interested parties, including teachers and local authorities, to be consulted on a regular basis.

A central unit serving regional teams seems to work well. If any particular 'strengths' are to be singled out, then the French national agency '*Service de la Formation et Administration*' has developed an excellent 'bank' of case studies and catalogue of training methods, and the Swedish team have done a great deal of work on evaluation of training programmes. Both centres give training, documentary support and an evaluation service to their regional teams. In Denmark, the new course for *folkeskole* heads will be based at the *Kommunale Højskole* (local government training centre) in Grenaa, which has already achieved a high reputation. The full-time number of staff running the course has teaching experience and will draw on help from the *Danmarks Laerer Højskole*, the headteachers' union, and some army psychologists. In Norway, various initiatives are being taken by various national councils for education and by the Kristiansand Teacher Training College. What is striking, however, is the way in which information and experience are exchanged down well-established informal grapevines in Norway. There is also a trend for the various agencies to work together, for example the national councils for the comprehensive *grundskolen* and the upper secondary schools are planning a joint programme. In all the training programmes there is an attempt to combine the experience and skills of full-time trainers and part-time practitioners who, in the words of an SFA trainer, can be '*pragmatique*'.

Course content

In content and emphasis the developments in Europe reflect the trends and fashions from across the Atlantic that have influenced our own training initiatives in Britain. Initial attempts at training provided 'administration' courses for heads, and then the emphasis changed to more general leadership, group work and human relations themes. There are signs of a stronger 'admin' emphasis in the French programme since SFA took over from its predecessor, INAS (*Institut National d'Administration Scolaire*), and in all programmes there is an attempt to get a proper balance of administrative and human relations training.

The greatest difference in approach stems from the degree of decision-making devolved to the school. In a system which provides detailed 'rules' for the head, administrative training is prominent. This is so in Danish upper schools (*gymnasia*) where a new course was instigated in 1980 concentrating on 'admin' problems for heads who have several volumes of regulations to understand. In contrast I encountered an excellent example of the organisational development approach in Norway in the County of Hordaland, near Bergen. This programme is based on ideas developed in the USA, the UK, and elsewhere in Europe. The training of the head is an integral part of an organisational development (OD) programme for the school to which all the staff are committed. This course lasts three years and begins with a typical OD analysis of the school which leads on to agreed priorities for development and innovation. The training of the headteacher takes place in the context of this programme, and in the last year schools begin to link together for contained mutual support as 'schools in contact' (SIK). This programme makes massive demands on the consultants running it. They require extensive training and are needed in large numbers – 25 consultants are needed in Hordaland for the training programme and a further 15 to cover the work with 'schools in contact' – all this for 200 *grundskolen* with between three and 50 teachers in each.

Between the extremes of a 'given' administrative training and the OD approach, there are many variations. The Swedish programme puts its main emphasis on the work of the head and his deputy in 'developing' their school, and the success of the course depends on the degree to which the head does his homework and involves his staff. In the Netherlands the course encourages heads to meet in local non-residential sessions to consider school problems. It was interesting to note that the 'long' course I visited in France, which was run by the Académie of Nantes-Rennes, also put emphasis on the need for the head to 'develop' the work team of all teachers, and not only the formal leadership team.

The resources put into training vary considerably. The Swedish course for school leaders is the largest, being a programme of 25 days over a period of two years and divided into eight residential sessions of three to four days. To this must be added four weeks of 'society-orientated' practice. Substitutes are provided for heads for all these days and in addition the head is given ten per cent of his working week, or half a day a week, to do his 'homework'. The total investment amounts to the cost of the course *plus* 82.5 full days of substitution – more costly than a three-month residential management course. The French investment in training is also considerable, with over 20 days in residence and an average of two weeks of practical observation. In the Netherlands the course is recognised as a 'survival kit' and the trainers are developing follow-up courses for those who have attended the initial 13-day course which provides for two periods of four days in residence.

Whatever the variations for all these countries, the training of heads and deputies is considered worthy of a substantial investment. The Danish course at Grenaa also provides for a basic course of four residential periods, totalling 21 days plus three more residential sessions over a total period of four years, whilst in Norway provision has been reduced from four to eight weeks in residence to a more modest, but still substantial, 15-day course for *grundskole* leaders and a '100 hours' course for those in upper secondary schools. Length of course is important if training is not only to improve the 'performance' of the head, but to make changes in the schools which are seen as beneficial by pupils, parents and teachers; and residential sessions are considered an essential element by all the trainers I met.

Evaluation

Most training programmes have been evaluated traditionally, i.e. participants and trainers have been asked by questionnaire or in discussion to comment on the course itself. In Sweden and France the total programme has been evaluated by an observer. The real problem is evaluating the effect of the training on the participants and their schools. Very little work is being done on this aspect, except in Sweden where the school leader education team at Linköping have analysed the results of a questionnaire to over 500 school leaders which indicates, even with cautious interpretation, positive results in the schools. (It also indicates that results are most positive where the trainer adopted a more questioning and active guidance role when helping the head to apply his training in the school.) The Swedish team are now embarking on a five-year evaluation which will look at a number of schools at the commencement of the training course and again after two years and five years. The work at Linköping could be of considerable help in moving towards a more reliable form of evaluation.

I did not spend much time discussing the issue of 'qualifications' or 'accreditations' for headship. All courses were careful to avoid evaluation of the participant who needs to be given confidence in his training to try improvements in his own school and his own performance as school leader. The one exception is the new course at Kristiansand: this gives 'credits' which will have salary implications and provide a 'pass' or 'fail'. The course has been under heavy fire from teachers' associations for this reason. Elsewhere this approach is avoided. In France, for example, training does not form part of the teacher's assessment for inclusion on the *liste d'aptitude* for promotion.

Trainers I met were keen to emphasise the need for heads to have a part in planning their own training. This is important at strategic level when the course programme on offer is planned, and at individual level. The Rennes Académie has developed procedures for negotiating course content with trainees, and in all the programmes which encourage participants to initiate development programmes in their own schools there is an attempt to meet individual needs. Training programmes must have the flexibility to help the head develop his own strengths and allow his colleagues to assume leadership roles in the school. Training schemes have to be considered in the wider context of national and local frameworks and support structures. The most convincing training programme I saw was designed to meet the needs of individuals and schools within the context of a properly orchestrated support structure and framework. Ideally, the rules, regulations, personnel policies, advisory services and systems of resource allocation, should be designed and shaped as far as possible to accord with the objectives of freedom of action for the school team and its leaders.

Important developments have occurred since 1980. This serves to underline the fragile nature of any comparative study. The position at the beginning of 1984 can be summarised as follows:

Sweden   The general provision for in-service training has changed radically. Voluntary attendance at in-service courses, team training and the provision for five (compulsory) study days for teachers in schools, have all been superseded by new arrangements. In-service education funds have been allocated to community (*kommun*) boards of education for in-service teacher education and local development projects, such as curriculum innovation. Sixty to eighty per cent of funds is used for INSET. This change now means that universities have to meet local needs. The six INSET institutes inside the universities no longer have nationwide subject responsibilities, but have responsibility for all aspects of INSET in their region. The regional board (*län*) responsibilities are gone, and inspectors at that level now act as resources for small *kommuns* and coordinators of INSET on request. The team training (*PLAG*) no longer exists in its original form. Such training is now a *kommun* responsibility, with help and funds from county (*län*) level as requested. The school leader education (*SLUG*) has also been modified. There are now only 20 residential days, not 25. Periods of home study are now 45 days equivalent, and are based on work in teams or groups, and not individuals. Society experience has been reduced from four weeks to one week, but visits at local level have been extended, involving local trainers much more. Of the total 45 days' home study, about 25 are given to the work done by an individual school leader in his own school. This work is now backed up by group non-residential day sessions. These changes have all taken place in the light of evaluations of the school leader training and seem to have resulted in much more effective utilisation of home study periods.

Norway Significant developments have also taken place in Norway. In Hordaland there has been an evaluation of the existing programme in 1981, as a result of which some changes have occurred, i.e. higher priority to innovation processes at school level; revision of the analytical methods used in the school to help teachers use them; a decision that the head and two teachers participate in the headteacher training programme; course themes to include pupils and the teaching process; and separation of the study and school-based innovation. In 1981 a nationwide innovation project was launched. The project is administered by the school director in each county in conjunction with the National School Council (*grunnskoleradet*) at national level. This project is similar to the Hordaland project but it is organised in different ways in each county. In Hordaland this scheme was based upon previous experience in the County. Under the new scheme the school director is responsible for consultant training. The time allowed for the seminars has been extended from one to one-and-a-half years to give more time for reflection and a more thorough introduction to the training. There is a significant shift of emphasis from 'cooperation between teachers and the planning of work' to 'cooperation in the classroom and educational development'. There is more emphasis in all themes on *pupils*. Administrative training is now provided separately for new school leaders at an independent course. There is greater realisation in the new programme that changes in schools come about gradually, and that each school has its own specific problems to tackle. The project evaluation continues and there is greater room for local variations. However, the two main change stratagems remain – leadership training and the innovation process in the school.

Denmark The course for *folkeskole* heads in Denmark is now becoming established, although it has experienced some difficulties because of the problem of funding participants at the introductory stage. Having a lower number of participants in the early stages of training has made it difficult to recruit sufficient numbers each year for more advanced stages. Heads of the 16-plus schools (*gymnasia*) have now special one-week management courses provided. Several counties also plan short courses of a similar nature.

The Netherlands   In the Netherlands the role of the training agency at Arnhem has now extended considerably. The Gelderse Leergangen is now called *INTERSTUDIE*. A small institute of school organisation and educational management (*INTERSTUDIE SO*) provides a well-established package of various training programmes. The team has now grown to eleven full-time members of staff. The basic course for heads is now one of six programmes offered by *INTERSTUDIE*. The other courses are:

- A course for management teams from colleges of education (primary education)
- A course for heads of department from institutes of higher vocational training
- Systems training for school management teams in secondary and higher vocational education
- A personnel management course also for members of school management teams in secondary and higher vocational education
- A course for women teachers who have an ambition to seek a school management career.

In 1984/85 two further programmes will be developed. One of these will be for recently appointed school leaders and another will provide training on the management of school mergers. *INTERSTUDIE SO* is now developing with a research institute a set of instruments for systematic evaluation of courses.

France   In France a new project is designed to give the school *conseil d'établissement* a large autonomy. This board, composed of parents, school personnel and members of the local community, would leave the head and his team executive responsibility for the school, but take on the role of liaison with the Ministry. This development of autonomy for the school could mark a significant change in the role of the *chef d'établissement*.

From 1985 a scheme of decentralisation in France will have considerable impact on present arrangements. A decree of May 1982 had already created a post in each *académie* for coordination of all training needs. The essential role is to bring together all existing training resources and to develop new training opportunities. So far these new arrangements have not impinged on headteacher training, but they will do – not least because of the impact of the overall decentralisation programme on the schools and on the basic administrative structure of the education service. The changes which are about to take place will fundamentally affect the scene I described in 1980.

Selection

Selection of heads was a subsidiary study. Most people I met envied the British promotion ladder in secondary schools and were complimentary about our selection procedures. One interesting fact that emerged from my visit was that Britain appeared to be ahead of the field in its selection procedures. Some differences in selection procedures were attributable to special factors:

(a) Small countries often dispensed with formal interviews because they tended to know the applicants;

(b) Industrial legislation, the fashion for participation by teachers, pupils, parents, has led to a sophistication of selection procedures. Preoccupation with 'democracy' has lengthened the selection process – in one Dutch municipality it now takes up to eight months to appoint a head.

Throughout the various countries, however, teachers have been worried by the trend to put selection into the hands of lay people, even where professional educators and members of elected school boards have retained a final veto. I was sorry not to visit Luxembourg which has the following simple procedure for selecting a head: '*Le Directeur d'un établissement d'enseignement secondaire est nommé par le Grand Duc sur avis des professeurs d'enseignement du dit établissement*'. If this succeeds, it calls into question all our interview techniques, personnel profiles and job descriptions. An example of somewhat broader involvement by the community may be seen in Haarlem. Here a new experimental headteacher selection scheme enables pupils, parents and teachers to draft preliminary views on the needs of their school and involves them in the preliminary stages of interview.

From my enquiries I am not convinced that selection is the major problem. Some countries have great difficulty in encouraging teachers to apply for headships, and *recruitment* is the major task. It is apparent that many suitable and qualified applicants need encouragement to apply for more senior posts. There have been some particularly successful recruitment campaigns in Stockholm which have encouraged teachers to apply for school leader appointments. There are many people capable of doing this job – indeed many people grow in the job after appointment. Selectors are very cautious about their ability to 'spot a winner', and selection techniques are by no means perfected. A good candidate for one school may be less good for another school with its different problems and circumstances. The most fruitful developments may be where an attempt is made to analyse the leadership needs of a school at the time a vacancy arises. A broad job description and personnel specification might then be prepared with these special needs in mind. Again, it is important to sort out the role of the lay person and the professional. There is a great deal of work the lay person can do to build up a picture of what a school and a local community expect of a head before the job is advertised. There seems to be less merit in involving various lay representatives in those stages of selection where a professional judgement of a candidate's ability is required.

The 'POST' project, the DES-funded Open University project on the selection of secondary headteachers, has subsequently provided a detailed study of selection procedures in England and Wales. In my view it is unfortunate that selective reporting of its findings failed to accentuate the positive. Although we have a great deal to do to improve matters, best practice is very good indeed. I hope that the 'POST' project conclusions will be carefully studied and perhaps discussed with others involved in a similar analysis of procedures in other European school systems.

International cooperation

When I set out for Europe in January 1980 I knew that at least one of the AEC Trustees hoped to see the possibility of a coordinated training programme for heads in Europe. In response I produced the following unhelpful conclusion: 'National structures and circumstances are so varied that the idea has no support. It would be difficult to agree a common core, even though many of the basic problems, pressures and needs are similar.' I did go on to propose, however, that 'the EEC might provide useful opportunities for trainers to keep in touch with developments elsewhere in Europe and throughout the world, especially in the USA, Australia and Canada'. I thought occasional European conferences on school leader education, involving contributions from all over the world, might help to give some impetus to our European training initiatives. And I felt it might also help if EEC bursaries enabled trainers to look beyond the confines of 'The Nine'.

It was the encouragement of the then head of the International Relations Branch at the DES (John Banks) that drew me into first-hand experience of coordinating international effort, and the three years since the study have made me test out some of my ideas – a frightening prospect for any armchair critic. I have selected two major areas of international activity for analysis here – a conference at Gatwick in March 1982, and UK participation in the OECD 'International School Improvement Project' (ISIP).

The idea of the Gatwick conference arose from my wish to provide teachers' associations in the UK with information on developments in other European countries. The first problem was to make sure funds were available and that people involved in training provision could be gathered together without encountering the usual problems of having 'representatives' of countries who might be remote from the subject and not wholeheartedly committed to the task in hand. First of all, a fruitful partnership was forged between the National Association of Head Teachers (NAHT) and the Association for Teacher Education in Europe (ATEE) which has its headquarters in Brussels. The final conference planning group came from three teachers' associations (NAHT, the Secondary Heads Association and the Assistant Masters and Mistresses Association) and ATEE. Conference organisation was in the hands of Pat Sharpe, then Assistant Secretary and Training Officer of the NAHT. Funding came from the EEC for those attending the conference from other countries, and the DES contributed towards conference expenses. The conference was attended by 60 people from nine European countries, and the majority were providers of headteacher training, from local education authorities and higher education institutes, heads or senior teachers and HM Inspectorate. Through the conference report, and a number of personal contacts which were forged at the conference, a great deal of information and a useful exchange of ideas was brought about through this 'once only' cooperative effort.

One disadvantage of the effort was its lack of sustained follow-up. Nevertheless, there is a useful place for events of this kind. Often people have been deterred because it is believed that funds are not available. By combining financial and human resources from the EEC, DES and teachers' associations, it was possible to launch a major event on a relatively modest budget. Much international activity is confined to a restricted number of experts, and 'findings' rarely get transmitted in understandable language to people who can act upon them. The current OECD 'International School Improvement Project' is one example of an international study which is designed to involve teachers, heads, trainers and education administrators together in collaborative studies. One aspect of the project is to do with school principal (head) training. UK involvement in this project arose because I was urged by John Banks to prepare a UK submission to the OECD. In 1981 the Dutch authorities had already prepared a school improvement project. Simultaneously a small group of people from the Society of Education Officers and the European Forum prepared a proposal for a series of international exchange seminars on the subject of headteacher and senior staff training. The UK proposal became merged with the broader-based Dutch 'school improvement project'. A major area of study entitled 'school leaders and change agents in the school improvement process' is linking various institutions in co-development activities in 14 countries around the world.

In June 1983 visitors from various countries looked at four examples of headteacher training programmes in England. It was a salutary experience to answer searching questions from experienced trainers coming from a different context. One British trainer was asked what the greatest outcome of his training programme might be. This question, from a Swedish observer, was answered as follows: 'The creation of a network of contacts for secondary heads who often feel isolated'. 'Then why run the course when all you have to do is forge a network?' the observer asked.

In 1984 the co-development opportunities of the International School Improvement Project (ISIP) will provide an excellent example of cooperation. The Swedish trainers from Linköping and the Dutch team from Arnhem have planned a seminar for trainers which may be hosted by the Bavarian authorities. The Swedish and Dutch teams have already visited each other and undertaken detailed study of training methods and approaches. Between them they are seeking the competence to 'arrange educational programmes that make school leaders aware of their role as leaders of the development work in the school'. They have already developed several training methods which can help school leaders (heads) to fulfil a development role in their schools. It is expected that trainers from many countries, including the team from the National Development Centre (NDC) for School Management Training at Bristol will participate in this seminar. The financial and human resources of two major training agencies and a state government will provide an opportunity to develop the effectiveness of training programmes. The idea of 'co-development' can be seen working at various levels. Writers in four countries are preparing a comparative study of the role of the school leader. A major agency in the USA has prepared a summary of literature and research into 'effective' headship. Several countries and institutions which are developing new training initiatives now have a network of personal and institutional contacts which can provide them with advice and support.

Finally, the International School Improvement Project is opening up contacts between countries which have been developing similar initiatives in isolation. Participant countries as widespread as Japan, Australia, the USA, Canada, Italy and the UK have the opportunity of pooling resources and ideas for key areas of research. It is hoped that ISIP and other international initiatives might forge useful links between providers and recipients of headteacher training. The OECD project is looking at the role, function and training needs of school principals and at the objectives, organisation and evaluation of training programmes, strategies and methods. We have much to give to, and gain from, cooperation with others.

Headteacher training in England and Wales

In my 1980 report I entered a plea for something to be done to coordinate efforts and provide desperately needed help. Since 1980, the Hughes Report and a DES initiative have come to pass. It is useful for me, and I hope for the reader, to compare the following comments I made in 1980 with my current analysis that takes on board these later events and brings this account of headteacher training up to the position in 1984.

1980 assessment

Training initiatives in England and Wales seem to be better known in Europe than here. The size, fragmented and devolved nature of our education system makes it difficult to achieve a sensible exchange of information and may be responsible for our inability to make a real effort to achieve widespread training opportunities for heads. It would be superficially attractive to spread our most successful initiatives to all parts of the country. The fact that we have failed to do so may be a symptom of a more fundamental problem and we shall not 'cure the measles by putting ointment on the spots'. Perhaps we still cherish the image of the autonomous head able to carry all before him – including the trembling parent – and blessed with the ability that any sensible chap has to cope with everything that comes his way. In reality, the freedom of action of the head is already being eroded by education and employment legislation, falling rolls, diminishing budgets and demands for participation and accountability. The untrained head, however experienced, now has many minefields of our making which he has to negotiate with care. His task is more complex in human, as well as in administrative, terms and we would do well to monitor the undue stress which now forms a normal part of the head's task. We ought also to see how far heads have been able to use the staffing structures in our schools to give real responsibility and staff development opportunities to their colleagues in these circumstances. The needs and problems of the English head look very much like those of heads in the countries which have taken major training initiatives. If the role of the head is changing rapidly, we must change our ideas about his support and training needs.

I have some final comments on the training methods I saw, and a possible structure for a national scheme of training for heads. The schemes which train heads in the context of their own school's requirements and link training to developments in the school, seem more likely to produce improvements which are apparent to pupils, teachers and parents. If real development is intended, training must involve 'the school', ie all members of staff who wish to have a hand in improving the performance of the team of the individual teacher.

People grow in the job and we are not likely to have heads 'on approval' or on a 'sale or return' basis. A probationary period for headship would affect the confidence of the probationer who needs confidence and security to perform well. Whatever the content of training, it must build confidence. The best courses help a head to develop his own strengths and use to the full the abilities of his colleagues. Where a training course provides some opportunity of involving all the staff, and not just the head or the inner circle of leaders, then there is more chance of a genuine and sustained improvement. The problem is that courses of this type require trainers who have credibility with heads, the skills for the job, and the time to maintain links with a school and its development over a considerable period of time. This is where we may have to pool our local education authority and higher education resources, rather than perpetuate the tendency to have training agencies bidding against each other in the auction room.

I began my study by assuming that secondary heads and deputies need to be trained separately from primary heads, education advisers and administrators. I have seen enough of heterogenous groups to be convinced that there is every merit in training together the various heads of our education services. If training is to lead to improvements in the classroom and new initiatives outside it, we have to consider training administrators, advisers, primary and secondary heads, community officers and others together for at least part of their training programmes. The results are not always comfortable. At least one Swedish school director has had to improve his communications with schools as a result of a free and frank discussion with fellow trainees.

Who should provide the training? A national staff college has been suggested, and Coombe Lodge offers a possible model. To meet the needs of English schools would require a larger and costlier institution. National staff colleges carry status, but a single national providing institution would fit neither the size of the problem nor regional variations. It would be difficult to sustain proper follow-up, and there is always the risk that a national institution would soon become remote from the real needs of schools. In my view it is better to coordinate existing resources on a regional basis, using boundaries that fit local circumstances and find local agreement. We already have some experience of regional training schemes through which we can develop a more coherent and sustained response to training needs. In a regional structure it would be possible to combine the skills of the professional trainers and the part-time practitioner trainer, as has been done in France, Sweden and Norway. A properly established regional network could provide the best features of the school leader 'powerhouses' I visited. The regional team's brief would include: training of trainers; preparation and exchange of training materials; evaluation of training programmes and their effects in schools; research into training needs.

The school leader training should ideally be suited to the general INSET coordination machinery. Coordination rather than coercion is required, however. But LEAs, HE institutions and teachers' associations would at least undertake to develop their own initiatives within the context of a discussion of training needs and developments in the region. In the context of a regional scheme LEAs might more easily be able to review the effect of their own support and policy structures on schools developing their own leadership through the training programmes. 'Public authorities must impose the right conditions for the development of the autonomous school'. (Dutch Catholic Schools Council Report on *The Autonomous School* February 1979.)

It would be necessary to make sure a formal structure existed nationally to enable regions to exchange views, ideas and experiences, to farm out major research tasks, and to improve our monitoring and study of school leader training in other countries. The National Foundation for Educational Research also offers a useful vehicle for the exchange and dissemination of written material.

This is just one possible way forward. It is vital that the debate is moved on to the stage where some positive decisions can be taken.

The picture in 1984

Although 1984 is here, I would contend that 'Big Brother' is only just beginning to 'coordinate' us. I welcome the development of the National Development Centre, not least because it should not fall into the trap of trying to duplicate the efforts of existing providers, and could provide a lively forum for national effort and international cooperation. Provision for training in school management for heads and senior staff in England and Wales has developed in a variety of ways since the late 1960s. A gradual development of award-bearing provision leading to Diplomas and Master's degrees has given new opportunities for some people. Other shorter course opportunities have included HMI *COSMOS* courses, DES regional courses, provision by teachers' associations, and provision by some regional LEA consortia, the first of which developed in the North West in 1972.

In 1980 the Hughes report revealed a varied but patchy provision. A report from a Society of Education Officers' working party confirmed the same picture. Some local education authorities had developed extensive opportunities for training, but many had not. The year 1983 saw the DES initiative in school management training which attempts to build upon the existing varied pattern of provision in higher education institutions and LEAs. The aim of the initiative is to achieve a systematic and more evenly spread pattern of school management training. DES Circular 3/83 outlined the major elements of the initiative: one-term programmes, 20-day courses and a National Development Centre at Bristol. The NDC is a joint enterprise between the University of Bristol and the Bristol Polytechnic South West Regional Management Centre. Its Director has stated that it is not a staff college, but a 'facilitating, supporting and evaluating' team with the daunting task of helping senior staff in schools – about 130,000 potential clients. The basic aims of the NDC are to improve the provision and effectiveness of management training for heads and senior staff in primary, secondary and special schools in England and Wales. It must be emphasised that the NDC is concerned not just with heads, but with middle management and the staff as a whole. Primary schools were recognised to be very different, and the NDC team anticipated that primary management training would also have specific needs.

The National Development Centre has five functions:

1. *Information collection*: to find out about good practice and collect material for a resource bank. It is envisaged that audio-visual, as well as paper materials will be collected, as will materials from overseas, industry and non-education management.

2. *Evaluation*: the NDC team are not inspectors. They hope to work collaboratively with institutions. They could only evaluate a sample of the courses; it would probably be possible to do a systematic evaluation of only one or two a term. However, they would encourage people to work with them to develop their own evaluation research kits. For example, particular individuals might come and work at the NDC for a term, possibly using 3/83 money, working on an evaluation kit or on materials for training in staff development.

3. *Development*: the team hope that with the assistance of people round the country, they could identify major gaps in the existing materials and develop some training materials in these areas. They anticipate that they will be working from their own strengths in the first instance, e.g. school self-review, staff development.

4. *Dissemination*

5. *Support for implementation*: the team realise that it is not sufficient just to disseminate. Support must be provided for implementation. However, the implementation phase began before the NDC was set up. The NDC has to work out a coherent policy for working with

LEAs, providing institutions, etc. The NDC staff as a group have diverse but complementary strengths and, in addition to their specialist roles, they have each taken on a regional responsibility.

The way ahead

What then are the issues to be considered by the variety of agencies involved in this field in England and Wales? There are massive gaps in the present state of knowledge and numerous problems in the working context of schools and heads which should influence anyone who believes there are instant solutions. One major problem that confronts the trainer is that of defining the job to be undertaken by the trainee. This is influenced by the nature of the organisation in which he works. The greater degree of autonomy we give to a school, the greater the task of the leadership team. The debate in the Netherlands on the 'autonomous school' has recognised that the school is only *relatively* autonomous, i.e. it has to work within the rules and guidelines laid down by external authority. It is common practice to change the rules without analysing the effect of the change on the school. In recent years heads have had to cope with legislation aimed at increasing participation by parents, staff and the general public in the life of the school. We have simultaneously given the head more responsibilities and invented prescriptions which limit his scope for action.

The job of the head has become more complex and stressful, not least because of the impact of financial constraints, consumerism, organisational and curricular change, and social changes. The head's job now seems to be a complex amalgam of leading professional and chief executive. The trainer's task is all the more complex if there is no agreement about the role of the head and no agreed view of his key tasks. Not only do we lack a consistent and universal view of the head's role, we also need to learn much more about *effective* headship if we are to provide training which has a positive impact on schools. First of all we have to define 'effective' – Do we want a chief education officer's 'yes-man', a governor's door-mat or a teacher's pet? Surely we require a school improver who is able to encourage school improvement.

School improvement was recently defined as 'positive and valuable changes in student learning outcomes, teacher skills and attitudes and institutional functioning'. We do not know what heads do that most contributes to school improvement. Indeed, there is a dearth of information on what heads actually do during the average action-packed school day. However, we can learn something from management literature. A useful summary of transatlantic literature is provided in a booklet produced by the National Association of Secondary School Principals in the USA. (*The Effective Principal: A Research Summary* – National Association of Secondary School Principals (1982), 1904 Association Drive, Reston, Virginia 22091, USA.) Certainly style of leadership matters, and effectiveness includes the proper management of time to allow for improving curricular and nurturing teacher developments, subordinating routine to its proper place, giving priority to external relationships, managing face-to-face relationships – including conflict – and providing a cooperative style of management. The key elements of effective behaviour need to be identified in order to nurture appropriate skills and encourage aspects of personal and professional development which will have positive impact in the school.

Once we have determined the role of the head, his key tasks, and have identified the skills and the style of management most conducive to school improvement, we still have to determine the relevance and role of training. Training has to be considered in the general context of personnel policies and staff development. It cannot rectify the mistakes of bad selection procedures, revive the walking wounded, or raise the dead. Staff selection, planned experience at various levels of management responsibility, pastoral and professional support to heads within an LEA, staff appraisal procedures and opportunities for job interchange, secondment and peer group networks, all have a place in developing and sustaining effective school leaders. Some UK training schemes have had ambitious aims, but little impact on schools. We have to be clear about the role of training. Furthermore, we need to have a clear, overall policy for the recruitment, selection, support, appraisal and development of school leaders if we are to stand half a chance of making the best of any formal training opportunities.

Once we decide that training is to be organised, there are many lessons to be learned – not least that of carefully defining the aims of training and the expected outcomes. Heads, or other potential 'trainees', trainers and employers have to build up a clear, agreed perception of the aims of a training course. Too often conflict of interests and perceptions have been left unresolved. In the Rennes Académie in France the idea of a training 'negotiated' by the various participants provided a good basis for an effective course. As soon as aims are examined rigorously, it is apparent that no course can meet through a universal programme the needs of each individual, each school or all LEAs. We do not even have a consistent method for recording the management experience and training already given to an individual. Basic information of this kind should be available.

It is the unique nature of each school and the uniqueness of each human being that presents trainers with an almost insoluble problem, once they attempt to 'improve' the school and 'change' or 'develop' the head. Some work in Ontario has indicated that the fruitful way forward might be to help a head to develop specific skills and strategies to overcome a particular obstacle to progress in his own school. The idea of 'profiling' has also gained some support. We should know for each trainee the management experience they have gained and the specific skills they have already mastered. This is an excellent idea, but cannot readily be achieved in England and Wales unless every one of the 104 LEAs develops a coherent scheme of staff appraisal and professional development. It might be possible to go some way towards this, however. One lesson to be learned is the importance of giving sufficient time and effort to clarifying training aims. Too often the recipients of the training, the employing authority and the training agencies can have differing perceptions of the likely outcomes. Many of these differences need to be resolved, or at least highlighted at the earliest planning stage. It is in this area that the established training agency may be most vulnerable. If a permanent building and permanent staff are to be maintained, it is possible that the objective analysis of training needs will be tailored to the needs of the training institution. Staff colleges need to secure regular staff changes by secondment, fixed contract or other devices if they are to combine a proper balance of experience in a particular training approach and healthy innovation.

Training strategies

Indeed, having determined the aim of training, there are numerous strategies and methods to be considered. Some of the most effective training agencies are deliberately avoiding adoption of a single approach. The training team at Arnhem in the Netherlands are providing custom built courses and training modules for complete task groups in schools, school management teams, project groups, steering groups, and people involved in major reorganisations or curriculum development. The timing of training may also be crucial. Individuals and groups may be most responsive to training when they are about to face a new challenge or development in the school. Much needs to be learned about the way in which heads learn. Heads learn best when they can learn through and apply adult learning methods with their own staff. They need a variety of these working methods in training, so that their own experiences are challenged. It is important to remember that all adults need considerable time to learn new skills and even more time to adapt attitudes and leadership styles. It is necessary to avoid programme overload. Adults need opportunities to gain confidence away from day-to-day pressures and responsibilities. Heads can be helped to improve communication skills, make better use of time, and improve their ability to delegate, if they are given appropriate learning methods and time for development.

There is much to learn about the evaluation of training programmes. Most evaluations focus on process and very little has been done to evaluate the impact of training on the school. A long-term project in Sweden is attempting this difficult task. I am not convinced that the impact of training can be evaluated in global terms. The schools under observation are constantly changing and it is virtually impossible to isolate the contribution of training to improvements in a school. Much more could be done, however, to monitor the impact of more detailed training objectives – to see, for example, how far heads have adjusted their management of time or improved specific areas of skill, such as chairing meetings or conducting interviews. It would be an important move forward if specific training packages, aimed at specific skills, could be developed. It is in this area that there is the chance of developing reasonably accurate assessments of performance improvement. This in my view would be a more fruitful evaluation strategy than attempting to evaluate the impact of training on that highly complex and ever-changing organisation – the school.

There is much to learn, and for this reason I consider it vital to devise an effective means of exchanging information on developments – both within the UK and across the world. The UK has much to contribute to the international effort. We have a varied menu of training approaches and training agencies. The Open University leads the field internationally in distance learning techniques for management training. The English headteacher still has considerable freedom compared with his colleagues in other countries who are now moving towards greater delegation of authority to schools. One important lesson emerging from my studies has been the degree to which teachers' associations, heads, advisers, education administrators, trainers and researchers *can* and *should* work together. From our various standpoints, we all know that *we* know best. Some of the best work, however, is being achieved by working together. Effective programmes will also seek to engage the skills and expertise available outside the education service. Perhaps senior students in schools also have a role – in defining in their terms what makes for effective leadership and management in the school as far as their present academic goals and future life prospects are concerned.

In a very small way we have now learnt the need for investment in senior staff training and development. This investment needs to be sustained and increased. Although we are late in the field with a national initiative, we have much to learn from the early initiatives, successes and mistakes of others.

Acknowledgements

I would like to record my special debt to John Banks, former Head of the International Relations Branch of the Department of Education and Science, to Cy Maxwell, formerly of the OECD, Ron Roberts, Assistant Director of Education for Schools, Avon, and Keith Watson, Lecturer in Comparative Education at the University of Reading. I could not have undertaken this task without the help of my programme coordinators.

I am grateful to: Ferry de Rijke, Ministry of Education, The Hague; Mats Ekholm, School Leader Education, Linköping, Sweden; Paul Lyngbye, Ministry of Education, Copenhagen; Aasulf Froeysnes, Ministry of Education, Oslo; and Roger Grandbois, Ministry of Education, Paris.

For their valuable help in updating my report for 1984 I have to thank: Jean-Pierre Helt, Inspecteur d'Académie, Rectorat Paris; Kaas Gielen, Director of Interstudie SO, Arnhem; Klaus Brodsgaard of the Communale Hojskole, Denmark, and Jorgen Olsen, Rektor of Fredericksborg Statsskole, Hillerod, Denmark; Eskil Stegö, School Leader Education, Linköping, Sweden; and Per Kvist, Director of Schools for Hordaland (Bergen), Norway.

Curriculum control

The days when a professional visit to Europe could ever be regarded as a junket with all expenses paid must surely be long gone, for time devoted to this purpose is much too valuable to waste. An initiative such as the AEC Trust Fellowship, involving three months of investigation abroad, reflects the importance of understanding and learning from our counterparts on the Continent. It gives an opportunity to make comparisons based on models and systems that have been tried and proven over several years in another country where circumstances are reasonably similar to our own. Without this element the whole exercise could well become nothing more than self-indulgence, a change to ride one's favourite hobby-horse. It would surely be an unwise commentator who would set out to offer opinions on matters so fundamental to the service without the comforting knowledge that somewhere not too far away, there are people no less rational than ourselves doing things differently and managing them rather well.

Personally, I found the experience more enjoyable than a holiday and yet more challenging than any administrative task that has so far confronted me. I firmly believe that this kind of enquiry should become recognised as an essential dimension in helping to clarify our thinking on the major educational issues facing this country.

Clive McNeir

Chapter 2

Curriculum control

Clive McNeir

Clive McNeir is Assistant Education Officer with Northamptonshire County Council. He took as the focus for his study of curriculum control the West German State of Hessen. After studying languages at London University, Clive McNeir researched into Renaissance French literature and taught at a French lycée. On his return to this country he taught at grammar schools in Gateshead and London, and joined the Inner London Education Authority in 1969. Six years later he took up his present post with Northamptonshire. One of McNeir's special interests is making educational films.

Changing course in Hessen

My interest in the control of the curriculum in the West German State of Hessen was first aroused in the early 1970s when, during a visit to friends living in that State, I happened to see reports in the press about some apparently far-reaching developments. I followed this up by seeking out a number of official publications explaining the new moves, and soon became involved in animated discussions on what should be taught and who should determine the shape and content of the curriculum. There was certainly no shortage of points of view on this topic and it was clearly uppermost in the minds of all my acquaintances in the education profession. What struck me most was the contrast between attitudes to the curriculum in all its aspects in West Germany compared with the UK.

Feelings ran high in Hessen and were sometimes expressed with passionate intensity, as the following quotation shows: 'I wish no-one the fate of President Salvador Allende of Chile. But if the seed which is being sown by the teachers and inspectors in Wiesbaden should flourish, one could only hope that even here there might be a few Generals who would plan an ungentle end to such progress with the help of those young people who have not yet been corrupted.' It seems hard to imagine any aspect of curriculum development in Britain arousing such a reaction as this. This bitter attack on new curricular guidelines being introduced in the State of Hessen was made by a professor at Frankfurt University in a newspaper interview in the mid-1970s. By then the controversy had been raging for several years and had already brought about the dismissal of the State's Minister of Education.

The highly political atmosphere in which curriculum development has been taking place in Hessen makes direct comparisons between our two systems rather tenuous, though it does illustrate how different countries determine what should be taught in their schools. During the course of my three-month stay in Hessen, I was able to meet nearly all the main protagonists in the conflict. We discussed their achievements and their failures and I came away admiring their determination to face up to the major issue of how to organise the curriculum. I also came away with a vivid impression of what can happen when the curriculum becomes fixed on the political agenda.

There are countless good reasons for visiting Hessen, even for those not wishing to carry out a study of the curriculum. Heavily wooded and blessed with large areas of outstanding beauty, Hessen has a mild climate where agriculture and viticulture thrive. It is a wealthy state, supported by considerable industry, such as Opel and Hoechst. The population numbers some 5.5 million with major centres at Wiesbaden, the state capital, Darmstadt, Frankfurt and Kassel. There are about one million pupils in schools. Hessen extends about 170 miles from north to south and 95 miles from west to east. The administration is organised in three tiers. The ministry in Wiesbaden, establishes policy. There are regional offices in Kassel, Marburg and Darmstadt to disseminate and co-ordinate policy. Day-to-day running of the schools is delegated to local education offices.

In Hessen, virtually all the ministry officials handling policy are members or supporters of the SPD (Social Democrats) or FDP (Free Democrats), the ruling coalition partners. This is not unusual and there is no secrecy about this. In the Federal Republic education is mainly the responsibility of the eleven states and city-states and the standing conference of education ministers, known as the KMK, helps coordinate policy.

The curriculum

The German attitude to the curriculum is quite different to ours. West

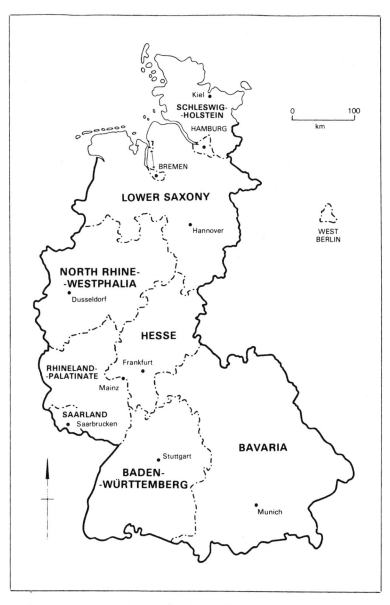

Hessen (or Hesse) in relation to the other lander of West Germany. This has been the political framework of West Germany since 1957. The map is extracted from 'West Germany: a geography of its people' by Trevor Wilde, published by Longman.

Germany has a written constitution and everyone knows their rights. So it is with the curriculum. Education is a right that the State, i.e. the nation, bestows on the citizen. The State therefore has the responsibility of determining what should be taught. Teachers, as employees of the State, have the duty of carrying out this task. In each State there exist prescribed syllabuses (*Lehrpläne*) broken down by subject according to the age of pupils and the type of school they attend. Thus, the teacher concerned with seven-year-olds will follow a syllabus in mathematics devised for that age group. The syllabus will have been developed by a committee appointed by the ministry and is backed by legal status. In most states secondary education is based on a tri-partite arrangement with the grammar school (*Gymnasium*) providing the most traditional academic education, the high school (*Realschule*) offering courses mainly for pupils who are unlikely to continue on to higher education, and the secondary modern (*Hauptschule*) giving a basic education to pupils expected to earn their living by practical work.

In most States this division between types of secondary school has to be reflected in the syllabuses. The teacher of mathematics in the grammar school will obviously be following a different course with a given year group from that being taught to pupils of the same age in a secondary modern. The problems that this can cause for the late developer who tries to move up to a more demanding school have been recognised for some time. Several states have begun to reorganise their secondary schools on comprehensive lines. Hessen went a step further and reorganised the curriculum, as will be described shortly, changing the emphasis from prescribed syllabuses to guidelines (*Rahmen-richtlinien*).

In theory, the schools' inspectors monitor what is taught. In practice, they are so inundated with administration that they have little time for this. Each inspector deals with 250 to 500 teachers. How often can they see them? The usual humorous answer is every three years for about half an hour. At the school level the onus of implementing the curriculum lies with each individual teacher, but before looking at their role a point must be made about headteachers. The German head does not wear the mantle of the English public school headmaster of the last century. He does not provide what we would recognise as 'leadership' or set out the ethos of his school. He is regarded as the first among equals and receives a supplement to his teacher's salary for handling administration. The head does not shape the curriculum, but dutifully passes on the continuous stream of administrative bulletins on this and every other matter sent out by the Ministry and the district education offices.

The German classroom teacher is at first glance much less free than his British counterpart. He is told what to teach with a limited choice of books approved by the State and he is subject to inspection. Yet he is more free than he appears. He can develop his own materials within the guidelines, inspection is infrequent and, most importantly, he controls the public examination (*Abitur*), setting and marking the papers taken by his own pupils.

Whereas in the UK the curriculum is heavily influenced by *external* examination boards, in Germany examinations are an important element in the curriculum management process. The system that I encountered in Hessen reinforces the professional responsibility of the individual teacher. The system works like this. The teacher of a class preparing to take *Abitur* examinations in his/her given subject area, prepares two papers which cover virtually the whole syllabus. These papers are sent to the appropriate school inspector who chooses which paper will be set. On the day of the examination, the papers are given out and the teacher has no idea which paper is being set until they are distributed to the candidates under examination conditions. The teacher then marks the papers completed by his/her own pupils and these in turn are passed to another teacher in the same school for independent checking. The inspectors have the right to call for the papers as a further check and are available to adjudicate in the event of any dispute or serious query. There is an established appeals procedure to which parents and pupils can have recourse if an unfair mark is thought to have been given. This is rarely necessary.

Under this system, the teachers play a key role which ensures that the control of a vital aspect of the curriculum remains within the schools sector and is not imposed from outside. Everyone I met was satisfied that the system achieved this degree of flexibility with adequate safeguards against abuse. The point to be borne in mind, however, is that this system works because it is underpinned by an agreed curriculum which is accepted by all the schools in the State.

At state level there is a Parents' Consultative Committee (*Landeselternbeirat*), to which all matters, including the curriculum, are submitted for approval. If a report is rejected, the Minister can only reverse this decision by taking the issue to a full debate in the state parliament.

1968: before and after

Before looking at the developments that took place in Hessen, it is probably worth reminding ourselves that the education service in Germany since the War has been marked by characteristics quite different from those experienced in other Western countries. Faced with the task of rebuilding a devastated country the watchword in education was 'No experiments!'.

Under the twelve years of National Socialism the education system had been directed centrally from Berlin and had become synonymous with authoritarianism and indoctrination. The new post-war republic returned to the devolved pattern that had been set up under the Weimar Republic. The system seems to have worked satisfactorily for two decades and was not seriously called into question until the movement for change and reform struck Germany, along with many other European countries, in the late 1960s.

The student demonstrations in Paris and elsewhere in May 1968 were echoed in Hessen at the University of Frankfurt. This caused great consternation to the State Government which had presided over stability and rising prosperity for more than ten years. The advent of a new State Prime Minister in 1969 led to the formation of a new Cabinet, with the Ministry of Education being offered to a 45-year-old professor of sociology at the University of Frankfurt. Until that time the new Minister, Professor Ludwig von Friedeburg, had had no political experience and was not even a member of the ruling Social Democrat Party, but was known for his ideas on democratising higher education.

'Without the unrest of 1968 I would never have become Minister', Professor von Friedeburg told me. 'I knew nothing about schools and spent my entire first year in office devising new structures for universities. Only then did I become aware that the schools, too, were in need of reform.' He realised that the situation was favourable to the introduction of new ideas. The economy was thriving, trade was expanding, pupil and student numbers were increasing and so, too, were resources. Above all, public opinion was ready and willing to accept innovation. There was a growing interest in what was happening in education outside Germany. Awareness was growing of changes of many kinds, and the words 'curriculum development' found their way into the German language.

It was in this atmosphere that a commission set up by the previous Minister of Education had been examining the need to change the curriculum, chaired by the eminent education specialist, Professor

Wolfgang Klafki of Marburg University. The commission numbered about 150 members, mostly teachers and academics, and was divided into three sub-groups working on projects to be tested in schools. The tests would have involved some thousands of teachers throughout the State, but before they could begin, the commission was abolished. Factions inside the Ministry wanted more control of the curriculum and persuaded the Minister that progress could be made more quickly and more economically if organised by the bureaucracy. Not one for half measures, Professor von Friedeburg then set up 25 smaller commissions, co-ordinated from within the Ministry, to look at each area of the curriculum and make recommendations. Now absorbed with comprehensive reorganisation, he left the commissions to do their work during 1970 and early 1971.

The new pattern was to be based on principles not previously followed in Germany. The Minister profoundly disagreed with the segregation of pupils into different types of school. 'All pupils have a right to a scientifically orientated education . . . the aims must be the same for all pupils because they are all citizens in a democratic society with the same rights and duties . . ..' There would be one curriculum for all pupils in a given year group, whatever their assumed ability. The tri-partite system would gradually give way to a comprehensive pattern by 1985.

From 1970 until he left office in 1974, Professor von Friedeburg set up 64 integrated comprehensive schools, far more than exist in any other State even today. But as far as the new curriculum was concerned, one problem followed another. The aim was to introduce new guidelines for trials in schools until gradually they were improved and made mandatory. Unfortunately, sensing that they were heralds of the new era, the commissions produced documents written in the latest sociological jargon in a style ranging from the arrogant to the aggressive. Many teachers found the new ideas unpalatable, particularly the more traditional teachers in grammar schools. Historians and geographers, for example, found their subjects abolished as separate entities and merged with sociology to form the new social studies (*Gesellschaftslehre*). The greatest emotion was aroused by social studies and German, which stressed mixed ability teaching and the social aspects of the language.

Hessen found itself projected in one leap from the curriculum of the 1950s, where geography dealt with the mountain ranges of the Alps or the tributaries of the Danube, into the very latest ideas on pedagogic theory and practice. Two examples will illustrate the controversy that resulted. The first is in biology, and is taken from the syllabus on sex education for pupils aged 11 years. This syllabus quoted 260 objectives on 54 pages. The act of reproduction was to be described in 38 numbered stages, using diagrams, film etc. In those children's homes there must have been some interesting conversations sparked off by the question: 'What did you do at school today, dear?'

The second example is in sport, where the syllabus amounted to some 12 pages, produced by a commission of 31 members. A fairly typical extract might read: 'The setting and differentiation of learning objectives in the motor, cognitive and affective spheres at various levels of abstraction . . .' etc. This style caused one headteacher to ask if the Ministry could provide a course in sociology for his PE staff.

I do not quote these in order to ridicule the work of the commissions. The guidelines contained many up-to-date ideas that were well established in other countries, but rather shocked Germany. Perhaps in trying to be too thorough they failed to achieve balance. But believing in the value of debate and discussion, the Minister took the courageous step of organising public meetings to put the case for the new system. These became a disaster, with rival groups chanting and waving banners like a football crowd. The television cameras were present and kept broadcasting live for the whole evening and past midnight. The Minister and his colleagues tried to keep the meetings going despite the uproar in an effort to raise the level of the debate. After three meetings this bold initiative in public consultation had foundered, thanks largely to the actions of extremist groups agitating for and against the changes being proposed. A genuine attempt to involve the people had degenerated into a kind of *'It's a Knockout'*. The end result was that the whole issue was trivialised and the policies lost much of their credibility.

By then it was 1974, the year of the State elections. The Social Democrats lost their majority and the Free Democrats agreed to a coalition, subject to certain conditions, including the withdrawal of the Minister of Education and the revision of his policies.

Getting back on course

According to the agreement between the Social Democrats and the Free Democrats there were to be no more integrated comprehensive schools established, and no more controversial guidelines. The Minister appointed to preside over this state of affairs was Herr Hans Krollmann, an experienced professional politician in his mid-forties.

It surprised me greatly during our interview that, even after six years in office, he still claimed to be no expert in educational matters. But on becoming Minister he demonstrated considerable political acumen, for he at once took firm control of the system. The more radical officials in the Ministry gradually found other appointments. The more radical members of the commissions were replaced. Nonetheless he has continued the process of reform in a manner that seemed impossible in 1974. He has doubled the number of cooperative comprehensive schools to over a hundred: these are tri-lateral schools on one campus under one head, with a common curriculum. Over 60 per cent of all pupils aged 10 to 12 years are in the two-year non-selective orientation stage in secondary schools. The aim is to achieve 100 per cent in this stage from the mid 1980s, and the Minister calculates that falling rolls will lead to greater demand for comprehensive education.

The curriculum commissions have continued their work, less controversially, and new guidelines have been introduced throughout the curriculum on a mandatory basis. Herr Krollmann has added a new dimension to curriculum development in two vital areas. Recognising that evaluation and the identification of changing needs must be built into the process he established in Wiesbaden in 1974 an Institute for Educational Planning and School Development (known by its initials as HIBS). Accepting the need for continuous in-service education of the teaching force as a vital means of support, he has improved and expanded the Institute for Teacher Education (known as HILF). Despite his professed inexperience in educational politics, the Minister was quick to recognise the need for an agency capable of identifying and implementing changes where they seemed to be required. Herr Krollmann readily secured the resources for ensuring that teachers received in-service training to equip them to meet the challanges of the new ideas. When discussing HIBS and HILF with the Minister, I was impressed by his realistic approach to the implications of change.

Today HIBS is responsible for producing materials, publishing details of new ideas and research, and evaluating the new syllabuses in the light of classroom experience. The materials I have seen are impressive, and there is no doubt that the teachers are taking an interest in them. The materials are well-presented and often pursue challenging themes; for example the course unit in social studies entitled 'Securing peace in the nuclear age. Theme: The neutron bomb'. The director of HIBS, Bernd Frommelt, and his colleague

Erika Dingledey who heads the Curriculum Development Branch, made it clear to me that they do not have a captive audience. They will only secure the support of the teachers if their materials are respected. 'Without the collaboration of the teachers, nothing will work', they maintain.

HILF has been based in Kassel since the late 1940s, occupying a magnificent wooded site surrounded by a bend in the river. As spacious and as well resourced as any college campus, it has expanded over the years with several branches scattered throughout Hessen. The number of branches is steadily increasing, despite the fact that expenditure cuts are being made. The teachers whom I met on courses at HILF clearly regarded it with respect, and the courses, covering a wide range of subjects, are always well supported.

Overview

As far as change is concerned, Hessen has achieved some successes. First, they recognised the need for change. They reorganised to meet changing needs with new structures capable of further development. They made resources available and have accepted a commitment to expansion in this area. They have implemented new policies aimed at harmonising the curriculum and school organisation, though political factors have prevented the completion of their plans. On the other hand, not every implication of change has been recognised. Control of the curriculum has remained firmly in political hands. The attempt has been made to introduce a more democratic system of control whilst retaining a rather autocratic bureaucracy. The role of the teachers has not been fully clarified, nor have the teachers been as fully involved in curriculum development as was originally planned. Finally, the reorganisation of schools has been stopped in mid-air leaving the new comprehensives in competition in almost every catchment area with grammar schools.

These shortcomings lead us to consider the question of political involvement. The education service in Hessen suffered considerable disruption, and in some subjects is still suffering, as a result of political interference in the curriculum. Even genuine attempts to promote serious public discussion were turned into shouting matches, and anxiety was aroused in the public at the apparent attempt by one party to use the schools as a means of spreading its views. There are clear disadvantages in having a curriculum management system controlled by a political institution. Not the least of these is that the imposition of a curriculum by a central authority is less likely to be capable of flexibility. Equally, if it did respond to the need for change, would it be guided purely by educational considerations? The dissolution of Professor Klafki's commission and the intervention of the Ministry alienated many teachers, parents and public opinion. There is little doubt that the politicians were swayed by considerations of speed and economy. The result has been the opposite of what they wished. This illustrates the problems inherent in seeking to impose a democratic process by autocratic methods, in seeking to impose curriculum planning from the outside instead of encouraging it to develop from the inside.

There has undoubtedly been some confusion at the teacher's role in Hessen, despite the continuous stream of directives from the Ministry. Some of this confusion has arisen because of changes in their role. Instead of working mainly alone with occasional reference to colleagues for the purpose of coordination, they are now enjoined to collaborate with other teachers, from other schools, in developing and evaluating the curriculum. Traditionally it has not been theirs to develop. Nonetheless, the creation of HIBS and HILF is evidence that the need to support and develop the teachers has been recognised.

Unfortunately the opportunity has not been taken to adapt the system at all levels to meet its new role. The inspectors have been allowed to remain inundated with a mass of routine paperwork, much of which could be handled by clerks. Headteachers, too, are burdened with administration and are not expected to lead discussion on curricular matters. As for the teachers, much of their confusion arose from being required to do too much, too quickly. The relative stability of the last few years, plus the increasing contributions of HIBS and HILF, have helped to clarify the position. But there is still concern from the teachers that they have not only had to work out new relationships with colleagues, but many have found themselves teaching new subjects, according to a new curriculum in a new type of school.

To a large extent the system in Hessen recognises the central role of the teacher. HIBS and HILF are staffed by specialists, though they do not have the freedom to determine their own policies. The Minister cannot contemplate relinquishing control in this politically delicate area. Of course, by seeking to placate public opinion in this way, the Ministry is arousing suspicion in the very sector which alone can make the system work. When I suggested to the Minister that HIBS might thrive if it were allowed to be independent of direct control by the Ministry, Herr Krollmann replied: 'HIBS *is* the Ministry. I cannot allow it to be independent. What they produce is only intended as a framework that teachers must fill in for themselves.'

The pressures on the curriculum and the demands of society are so great that it is gradually becoming clear that the teachers cannot be expected to take on this responsibility as they have in the past. In order to respond to these demands it is my view that we need a means of coordinating national policy. Already developments are taking place that will change the system quite fundamentally by the back-door unless they are checked. Whatever system is introduced for managing the curriculum, the experience of Hessen leaves me in no doubt that this body must be separate from political control. The most encouraging prospects in Hessen seem to lie in the work of HIBS and HILF.

It seems to me entirely appropriate that the curriculum should be regarded as the professional domain of the teaching establishment, but I do not believe society as a whole will any longer accept that it is the teacher's 'secret garden'. Teachers need much support and guidance in this difficult area. Equally, they must take heed of the demands of society.

Curriculum management in Britain

In setting out to unravel the controversial questions about managing the curriculum which emerge from the experience of Hessen, I bring the perspective of the education officer to bear on issues which have been explored by full-time researchers and other experts. I would like to suggest that this is no bad thing. If anyone is going to consider whether we should manage the curriculum in a different way, it seems to me preferable that this should be looked at by someone on the inside of the system acting objectively, rather than by someone on the outside who may be trying to make a political point.

Confronting the need for change is nothing new for the administrator in education, and this can help reinforce his objectivity. Despite being committed to securing the best education service at all levels, he is unlikely to be so attached to any one part of it that he cannot conceive of it being impervious to changing demands. The very facts of administrative life, where change is more or less constant, may have something to do with this. As administrators we are so used to facing difficult decisions about many aspects of the service which we might regard as indispensable, that we do not necessarily recognise a sacred cow when we see one.

Before considering what lessons may be learned from Hessen, and whether we in this country should be thinking more seriously about managing the curriculum in a different way, it may be noted that inertia seems to be the current response to any call to reorganise the curriculum today. In many parts of the service there are demands for a period of stability. It is argued that the comprehensive system should be left alone to settle down and sort out its problems without further tampering. Such views may be borne of real conviction - or complacency.

It is widely believed that the lack of a nationally operated system to control the curriculum is one of the strengths of education in this country. Because of the devolved pattern in which we work, the argument goes, there is no danger of interference from outside the school. Highly experienced commentators whose analyses are generally respected advance the conclusion that genuine curriculum development can only be initiated from within the school. Having been brought up in the system employed in England and Wales, I fully understand the spirit in which such statements are made. But, having had the opportunity to spend a period of time looking at how things are done in the States of West Germany, I feel bound to say that I think we could usefully take account of what our German neighbours do and why they do it.

It does not seem to me that effective curriculum development can only go on in school. Surely, the point about development is that it can take place anywhere. We have only to recall the initiatives of the Nuffield Foundation, the Schools Council, and departments in a number of universities sponsored by organisations such as the Ford Foundation, to recognise the value of such contributions in support of the teacher. To my mind it is doubtful whether, in these days of constraints on resources, the heads and their staff will feel sufficiently free from threat to embark on bold curricular initiatives.

In Hessen, the curricular resources developed by HIBS and HILF are in my view impressive. Most importantly, the teachers use them with confidence and success - not because they have to, but because they recognise their value as the products of much thought and expertise. This assessment is based on the quality of the resources themselves and the knowledge that many of the most experienced and committed teachers have been fully involved in their preparation and production. So it is, also, with the curriculum itself. In the work of the commissions formulating the overall education programme, the teaching profession is in the centre of all the work being undertaken, supported by the other members representing interested external bodies, whose involvement strengthens the whole undertaking. There is no question that this broad base undermines the operation. No teacher with whom I spoke resented this system; they welcomed the close involvement of those who were perceived to represent society in its many facets.

If it is accepted that curriculum development can take place in a variety of ways, there can be no doubt that curriculum implementation is only possible in the classroom. But this simple statement leads me to the opinion that we must look beyond the classroom and indeed beyond the individual school if we are successfully to manage a process of education that will serve the needs of future generations in any meaningful way.

Curriculum planning

In curricular planning terms is the school alone a viable unit for determining what is required to meet the aspirations of its pupils? On the face of it there would seem to be grounds for accepting that the school ought to possess the means of fulfilling this requirement. But do teachers need more support than their individual school can provide? Despite my admiration for so much of what is done in our schools, I find myself doubting whether the school has the capability of answering all the questions posed by the world in which we live, and whether we should expect schools to bear this responsibility with, as expressions of society as a whole, only the well-intentioned amateurism of their governing bodies to help them. For all the good work achieved in certain subject areas, we seem to lack curriculum models which look at the whole curriculum. There is much evidence that we are aware of this need, but for some reason we stop short of proposing solutions that may seem rather radical. If we recall the upheaval that was experienced when Professor von Friedeburg grasped this problem in Hessen in the early 1970s, this reluctance is not surprising. For all that, there is a clear dissatisfaction with the *status quo* among many teachers, but no evidence of leadership in this area.

It is easy to understand why many teachers are dissatisfied with the arrangements that exist at present. Teachers feel themselves to be under threat from so many sides. Parents are more vociferous and have been encouraged to be more demanding by recent legislation such as the Education Act 1980. Governing bodies are starting to ask more questions. HMI reports are being made public. And there are continuing demands from central Government for further restrictions on public spending. Those education authorities that have responded to the calls for higher standards and higher resourcing have quickly found themselves faced with the prospect of penalties being imposed from Whitehall. Who can blame teachers if they choose to keep their heads below the parapet and just get on with the job?

And yet, now perhaps more than ever, there is a real need for a comprehensive reappraisal of the whole curriculum. When times are difficult we should be looking hard at what we are doing to make sure we are going in the right direction. If we do not review the whole process, how are we to take decisions on those parts of the curriculum that are pressing for their place in the scheme of things? I am referring to such subjects as political education, conservation, highway education, philosophy and ethics, consumer education and peace/conflict studies. All of these have been considered by appropriate commissions in Hessen and in other German States and been allotted their place at a suitable point in the curriculum. During my AEC Trust Fellowship visit to Germany, for example, my daughter who was then aged eight had one hour per week of highway education at the local primary school in Heppenheim. The buildings here may have been erected in 1581, but the approach to education was geared to the demands of the modern world.

Does discussion about these competing pressures really take place in every school in England and Wales? If it did, it is doubtful where the resources would come from to enable the new developments to take place. Some of these questions caused the commissions in Hessen considerable heart-searching, but at least the questions were raised and debated. Where necessary the resource implications were identified and costed, and provision was included in the budget.

Teacher autonomy

British teachers are sometimes considered to be free from extraneous control, whilst their Continental counterparts are seen to be dominated by a state system that limits their initiative to innovate, to develop a personal style, or even to choose their own books. Our thinking on this subject is unduly influenced by the old joke about France, where, for example, geography teachers are all supposed to be on page 158 of their fourth-year prescribed text-book on 17 February. The point can be made from the experience in Hessen that, within the agreed guidelines, teachers are free to develop their own materials to supplement the texts recommended by their subject commissions. There is clearly much scope for exercising professional judgment. We in this country compare very favourably with Germany in the scope teachers enjoy to compile and implement courses. Where in my view we do not compare so well is in having less guidance and consensus on the direction of the whole curriculum. In this regard I find it worrying that our teachers are so isolated when so much is expected of them.

This dichotomy is nowhere more clearly illustrated than in the setting of public examinations. The system I have described in Germany places the teacher in the centre of the process, and the examinations are securely internal to the schools with safeguards to ensure unified standards throughout. In comparison, the British teacher in the upper reaches of secondary education is subject to syllabuses intended to identify aptitude for further study at university level. Any scope for reaching agreement on a whole curriculum model is bound to be constrained by this narrowly subject-orientated and specialised approach. It may be that a pattern of organisation more akin to the CSE boards, with the continued development of Mode 3 courses, could open up this sector to permit broad-based curricular initiatives, which would paradoxically be not dissimilar to the type of responsibility held by our German colleagues.

Whether we are considering examinations or the curriculum, the anxiety that exists behind all our thinking is that some sinister political force might somehow manage to take control of the process and exercise this power to indoctrinate our children with extreme views. This prejudice may seem healthily sceptical, though its origins seem to me unclear. Perhaps this is related to a desire to avoid the apparent excesses arising from the growth of fascism and communism in certain countries at times during this century. Or perhaps it is a feature of the growth of the teachers' associations seeking to define their sphere of operation and wishing to safeguard the scope of their members to claim professional status. Whatever the cause, it is paralleled in the Federal Republic by a similar wish to avoid centralisation for reasons already mentioned. In Germany there is, however, a recognition that a reasonable amount of political involvement in education is a further form of support, provided that the system has adequate checks and balances to prevent domination.

Central control

We have seen how the desire for changes in schooling was recognised by Professor von Friedeburg and his political colleagues around 1970, and how his successor Herr Hans Krollmann was able to build on the initial moves, despite a hardening of public opinion. Such intervention, praiseworthy though it was, would be unthinkable at the present time in this country in any matter concerning the curriculum. But how should we perceive the political role? Some would give this question a fairly brusque answer, but the question remains to be considered, for the first signs of ministerial interest in this sphere in recent times appeared in March 1981 with the publication of the DES document entitled *The School Curriculum*.

Since then, references to a national policy on the curriculum have proliferated, leading up to the speech made by Sir Keith Joseph in Sheffield in January 1984, in which he made specific mention, *inter alia*, of the need to adopt a different approach to both the primary and secondary curriculum. If the proposals made by the Secretary of State are put into practice, the direction of this key policy area will have been changed to an extent unequalled in recent times. The issue is not so much whether the Secretary of State should have a role in this area. It will be for him to decide what form this role should take. In historical terms the idea of not having a prescribed curriculum is a recent one, and we can recall that the nationally fixed syllabuses for primary schools were dropped in 1929, whilst those for secondary education remained in force until 1944. Nowadays it would probably be unlikely for the Secretary of State to attempt a complete takeover of the system. We would no doubt expect there to be a recognition of the partnership that exists in various forms between the providers, the client group and society in general. This was certainly the case in Hessen, where in particular the key role of the teacher was always fully acknowledged. The nature of the education process sets it apart, of course, from such political questions as defence or fiscal policy or the implementation of the EC regulations on the size of duck eggs.

So far, the recent political involvement in this country has expressed itself within the framework of the relationships established since the 1944 Education Act, referring to the need for Secretaries of State to work with 'partners in the education service so that their combined efforts secure a school curriculum which measures up to the whole range of national needs and also takes account of the range of local needs . . ..'

Nowadays, of course, the ranks of the partners have swelled to include the Manpower Services Commission, whose resources and consequent influence on certain sectors of education seem to be growing from one day to the next. The Commission's impact on the curriculum of some age groups has been phenomenal, and serves to underline the fact that real influence resides in the ability to mobilise investment. Whatever reservations the teaching profession might have about who should control the curriculum, there has been no shortage of applicants for MSC-funded projects.

The theme of partnership is reiterated in Circular 6/81, where reference is also made to 'the Government's policies which bear on the school curriculum'. But what if the Secretary of State decides he is not happy with the results of this appraisal? What sanctions could be involved? In Hessen the Minister believed he had no choice but to take direction into his own hands. We have no reason to believe that this would happen in Britain. But then we had no reason to believe the Secretary of State would abolish the Schools Council so soon after the Trenaman Report, commissioned by the Secretary of State, had praised its work and recommended its enhancement.

The point is that, whether or not we believe political intervention is possible, we must recognise that times are changing. The days are gone when Secretaries of State did not presume to trespass in the 'secret garden' where the teacher's responsibility was acknowledged as inviolate. It is now becoming routine for reference to be made in official documents to curricular issues, for example, the consultative paper on foreign languages in the school curriculum: '. . . The Secretaries of State intended to publish a statement of guidance on national policy . . .'. It is clear that the term 'partnership' is taking on a new meaning.

These changes can be faced in a number of ways. We can ignore what is happening, in the hope that this is a passing fad that will go away. We can man the barricades, proclaiming our belief in academic freedom. Or we can accept that our curriculum is in need of a new stimulus and seek new ways of improving it for all parts of England and Wales. The experience in Hessen shows what can be done when the teaching profession accepts this kind of challenge and a continuing commitment to keep matters under review. This course of action could retain overall control within the profession with invaluable support from outside. This could be particularly important when the allocation of resources is being debated. At the moment there is still a policy vacuum concerning the curriculum. Perhaps the demise of the Schools

Council will help concentrate our minds on how to fill this gap by building on our devolved system, before someone comes along with the weight and resources to fill it for us.

Planning mechanisms

The difficulty that we are facing in this regard is that no machinery for national curriculum review or development exists at the present time. But it is clear that changes are now taking place and new mechanisms will inevitably have to be devised in the light of these changes. It is my view that during this period of change we will sorely miss the wisdom and expertise of the defunct Association of Education Committees and the Schools Council. Furthermore, the new bodies, the Schools Curriculum Development Committee and the Secondary Exam-inations Council have yet to establish their presence on the scene. Without wishing to prejudge their future contributions, it does seem regrettable that the system should be further fragmented in this way, especially in two areas which are so fundamentally inter-related.

Do we need to consider whether commissions examining the curriculum should be set up in this country? They certainly appear to have worked very well in the German States, even in Hessen where political unrest threatened to cause the whole edifice to collapse. Yet we are faced with very different circumstances. We have 104 local authorities accustomed to determining their own policies. We have national bodies representing the shire counties and the metropolitan boroughs respectively that have been known to take differing stances on policy issues. We have no established mechanisms in this field at national level and no coordinating groups at regional level, apart from those relating to further education. All this does not seem very promising when looking for a way forward.

Should we then rely on the good sense and experience of the local education authorities? Their track record in this area is hardly impressive, since they have no background in curriculum management in any dynamic sense. Also, does the country really want 104 curriculum models? In his report on William Tyndale Junior School, Robin Auld QC made the point that in matters such as standards of attainment, specific aims and objectives and teaching methods, most LEAs have no policy. The popular view has been that teachers decide on what their pupils should learn since they know them best. Freedom to take decisions for oneself is splendid, but having no policy on such a fundamental issue does not seem to be a very satisfactory safeguard for the liberty of anybody. And where does accountability feature in all this? How do we ensure that our system meets our needs and is capable of responding to change? By what means does informed opinion take shape on how well we are achieving our goals when we do not appear to know where we are going? Are we now moving towards a national policy introduced by the Secretary of State, or will we drift into a core curriculum based on those subjects which lend themselves most readily to examination? Should we alternatively look for direction to the Department of Education and Science? Given our traditional devolved system, this would doubtless seem too radical a change to be acceptable to the educational establishment and it is unlikely that the Government would wish to embark on such a course where financial resources could prove extremely difficult to manage. It is also apparent that the three wings of the DES, the politicians, administrators and HM Inspectorate, do not necessarily share the same views on all topics.

Is there any other means of securing the kind of system that we need, and can Hessen give us any guidance in this? First, I hope and expect that our politicians will not be tempted to try to take control as Professor von Friedeburg believed he had to. Second, there appear to be certain advantages in the kind of regionalism embodied in the Federal Republic. Third, there must be recognition of the importance of the role of the teacher in terms of direct involvement in the planning process and in the commitment to a system of in-service education and curriculum review. In looking for a regional approach I have realised that some precedents do exist in this country. We are familiar with the Regional Advisory Councils in further education and the Regional Examination Boards for the Certificate of Secondary Education. The DES operates a regional organisation for administration and inspection purposes.

If there is no desire to adopt a national, centralised system for curriculum control and if it is considered that 104 separately developed curriculum policies involve a rather excessive amount of duplication, the notion of a regional approach has certain attractions. During the mid 1970s, the Schools Council began to develop a plan to establish 16 regional curriculum development centres throughout England and Wales. Unfortunately only four were set up and they have emerged as information centres. In my view we could usefully re-examine this pattern, which could claim to be potentially cost-effective when compared with reliance on numerous local arrangements.

I see little point in describing at length how regional curriculum planning councils/committees might work, for if the principle gained acceptance there are several ways in which such a policy could be enacted. Fundamental to the whole process would be the concept of collaboration between relevant parties. In Hessen the curriculum commissions included appointees from the trade unions, churches, employers' organisations, higher education and parents. These gave their advice and support to the representatives of the teaching profession. It would also be crucial to keep in view the development of the whole curriculum as well as individual subject areas.

If such a system were adopted, the LEAs would continue to play a dynamic role in support of local initiatives, especially in terms of their advisory and in-service teacher education functions. At school level, governing bodies would continue to bear the shared responsibility for reviewing the content and quality of education. Clearly, there would be major implications for the examination system and this would need to be considered as an urgent priority, for it is surely not desirable to regard these two areas in isolation from one another. The object of the exercise is to provide unity and conformity, rather than fragmentation.

Partnership

In my experience, virtually everything of importance in education has been determined through partnership, usually based on compromise. When I returned to Britain after three months in Germany, our system for managing the curriculum struck me as a kind of anarchy, with various new developments pulling in different directions with little apparent coordination. What had struck me in Hessen was that there the curriculum had often seemed too prescriptive; some of the guidelines were set out in too much detail, so that on paper teachers had only to follow orders to fulfil their contracts. But this was not by any means uniform throughout the curriculum. The teachers' common sense and professional judgment were important factors in making the system work. Taking these points into consideration, it remains my view that the *principles* on which the system is based in the Federal Republic are more conducive to the development and implementation of a balanced programme of learning, capable of meeting current requirements and possessing the flexibility to respond to future challenges than the process that we follow in England and Wales.

When looking at the achievements of other countries, it is all too easy to regard their grass as greener than our own and describe everything as some kind of ideal. Our colleagues in Hessen would laugh at any such idea and their reaction to my initial report was to regard it as fair criticism. It could be argued that there is no obvious reason why we should take special notice of how things are done on the Continent. If we tend to do things in a markedly different manner, it is because our traditions are based on different circumstances. But should we not ask ourselves whether we ought to be giving our teachers the kind of support that some other countries give? Do we believe that the other countries are all out of step and we are the only ones marching in time to the music?

At the time of my stay in Hessen, Chancellor Helmut Schmidt was urging the Germans to have 'courage for the future' ('*Mut für die Zukunft*'). With all the challenges we are now facing we need to recognise the problems and seek out solutions as a matter of urgency if we are to provide the best service to meet the needs of future generations. Having seen at first hand how one West German State has tackled its problems head on, I believe that we could do no better than to make '*Mut für die Zukunft*' our watch-word too.

Acknowledgements

I would like to express my sincere thanks for the help given to me by colleagues in Germany, especially Herr Hans Krollmann, Professor Dr Ludwig von Friedeburg, Dr Hans-Martin Schreiber, Herr Georg Rutz, Frau Erika Dingeldey, Dr Clive W Hopes, Professor Dr Wolfgang Klafki, Herr Helmut Bechtold and Frau Carola Port.

In Britain I received valuable guidance and support from George Cooke CBE and Eddie Lewis of the Society of Education Officers, and from John Mann and Maurice Plaskow.

For young people, perhaps the greatest challenge of our times is the competition for scarce employment. With renewed interest in the needs of the 14–19 age group it seemed that the education service in Britain could profit from an assessment of experience in Europe, and I used my AEC Trust-funded study visits to research policy and practice in Denmark, the Federal Republic of Germany, Sweden and France for the preparation of young people for working life. Completing the picture, given the trend towards a shorter working day and life, together with rising youth unemployment levels throughout Europe, I took the opportunity to look at measures in all four countries to prepare young people for greater leisure and at special programmes for the young unemployed. I also probed employers' views of their respective education services.

My report prompted meetings with Government Ministers, exploring particularly the links between education and training, vocational education in schools and student allowances. These may, I hope, have contributed something to current debate.

Michael Sweet

Chapter 3

Transition to adulthood

Michael Sweet

Michael Sweet, Deputy Director of Education, Solihull, used his AEC Trust Fellowship to investigate policy and practice in education and training for working life, leisure and unemployment in Denmark, West Germany, Sweden and France. After teacher training at Winchester and reading French at Rennes, Michael Sweet taught in secondary schools and further education for twelve years, including four as head of a military school in Northern Ireland. He entered administration in Warwickshire in 1969 and was appointed Assistant County Education Officer in 1971. In 1977 he moved to his current post at Solihull.

'The rest is silence'. Ernst Frederiksen at the Ministry of Education in Copenhagen borrowed from Hamlet to describe the plight of 20,000 Danish school leavers (or 20 per cent of the age group) in 1983 – the 'rest' group – who found themselves without work. My visits to Denmark, the Federal Republic of Germany, Sweden and France confirmed that all, unhappily, share our problem of youth unemployment, if to different extents. But I learned too that each has something to contribute to the common goal of improving the employment prospects of young people and of softening the worst effects of being without work, and also to the other theme of my investigation – the preparation of young people for greater leisure and a shorter working life. From the outset, the 16–19 limit proved unsatisfactory and in some places I have extended downwards to 14 and in others upwards to 26. Within this wider age-span I have been concerned throughout with four issues: curricular developments preparing young people for greater leisure and a shorter working life; the preparation of young people for the transition from school to working life; special measures for the young unemployed; and employers' views of the education service.

Preparation for leisure and unemployment

West Germany alone among the four countries has given thought specifically to the preparation of young people for increasing leisure. At the 'Courage to Educate' forum [1] in 1978 one of the nine topics debated was education as a non-vocational activity and as a preparation for leisure. In practice, however, little more has been achieved in West German schools than elsewhere. All four countries acknowledge the need to examine the whole question but more often than not my question was reversed! The idea of preparing young people for long-term unemployment caused offence to my Swedish hosts. Curricular developments are, in the main, unexceptional. Danish 14–16 year olds in the primary and lower secondary school (*folkeskole*) may choose from a list of 15 options which include film, photography, electronics, motor knowledge, and child care. In West German secondary modern (*Hauptschule*) and intermediate (*Realschule*) schools, 14–15 year olds follow compulsory courses in music and art, or textiles, whilst sport for three periods weekly is common to all types of secondary school. In the small number of comprehensive schools (*Gesamtschule*) where 'all day' timing has been adopted – 8 am to 4 pm – extra staff are provided to mount an impressive programme of structured activities in the afternoon session. A course in community studies is compulsory in the upper secondary school (*Gymnasium*) and options include geology and astronomy.

In the Swedish comprehensive school (*grundskola*), all 14–15 year olds take compulsory courses in home economics and child care, and craft courses in textiles, woodwork and metalwork. There is also a compulsory minimum of two periods weekly for extra-curricular activities. In the integrated upper secondary school (*gymnasieskola*) for 16–19 year olds, all 'lines' of study include courses in civics or job-world orientation and gymnastics, and a popular option is consumer education. In France, only physical education and sports are compulsory in all forms of post-14 education in the comprehensive school (*collège unique*) and the academic and vocational *lycées*; music and art subjects are compulsory only in some. Activities outside the school day but based on schools are notably well developed. Ten per cent of timetabled hours may be used for educational projects (*projets d'actions éducatives*) aimed at the enrichment of classwork; *colonies de vacances* and *d'hiver* are popular; and the well-organised clubs (*foyers*) attached to most schools make an important contribution to leisure interests.

Adult education in all its forms is extensively provided and well supported in all four countries. Denmark has gone so far as passing a Leisure Time Education (Consolidation) Act. Municipalities have a duty to establish youth schools for 14–18 year olds which offer a uniquely flexible approach to out-of-school education, both day and evening, in academic, vocational and leisure type activities. Folk high schools and other similar Scandinavian inventions contribute to a system from which 800,000 of the population of five million benefit. The main West German provider of adult education is the adult education college (*Volkshochschule*) with more than four million enrolments, but youth enrolments are disappointingly low. There is widespread popularity for one-off lectures or series of lectures on cultural topics and leisure pursuits. Non-authority provision through the churches, professional associations, radio and other media is well developed, and legislation in some States allows employees ten days' paid leave of absence every two years to follow approved general and cultural courses. Sweden's approach to adult education is particularly striking. Upwards of 14 per cent of enrolments in the integrated upper secondary school are adults, whilst a third of the adult population of five millions is engaged either in these school-based courses or in municipal adult education classes which are normally free, financed partly from the proceeds of a payroll tax. More than 300,000 subsidised study circles, 120 folk high schools and two adult schools make up the rest of adult education offered by a service that is outstandingly responsive to changing demands and circumstances. In France, *éducation permanente* is acknowledged as a powerful force. A great variety of voluntary organisations, such as *Peuple et Culture*, promotes courses, and universities are active in establishing study centres. The idea of the Université du Troisième Age – pioneered with the needs of the retired in mind – is likely to be extended to younger age groups. Youth information centres make effective links between provider and client, particularly in the areas of leisure and sport.

Transition to working life

It is tempting to over-enthuse about the approaches in all four countries to preparing young people for the transition from school to work. Each is different, but all are outstandingly successful in their own context. Throughout I have confined myself to the 14–19 age group. There is only passing reference to those forms of upper secondary education leading to university and other higher education as the route to working life.

In **Denmark**, the 14–16 curriculum in the lower secondary school includes a compulsory subject – contemporary studies, essentially an introduction to local and national affairs, and an option – vocational studies – which covers lessons in working conditions, expectations and environment, applied economics and training facilities, together with visits or training attachments to firms. The Danes acknowledge that there is a need to revise the vocational element in the curriculum; indeed, the radical suggestion was expressed more than once that, for some pupils, the pattern of compulsory academic subjects and optional practical activities might usefully be inverted. One interesting facility is the possibility of early leaving at 14-plus for young people who have the firm offer of a trainee post or work and who satisfy certain conditions. At 16-plus, students have two routes available to them. Approaching 40 per cent enrol on mainly academic courses in the upper secondary school (*gymnasium*). The growing surplus of academically qualified young people has unavoidably led to control in numbers proceeding to university and other higher education, and a *numerus clausus* system has operated since 1977 within 20,000 university entries annually. About 42 per cent of leavers enter the basic vocational education programme (EFG) for training which lasts three years. The contribution of this programme to the successful preparation for working life is undoubted. The basic, unpaid first year is full-time further education, for which each student selects one of eight broadly-based vocational areas – commerce/clerical, metals, construction, food, graphics, services, agriculture or transport. This is followed by two years as an apprentice or in other employment with associated vocational education. The outstanding features of EFG are that it avoids narrow specialisation, discourages uninformed career choice, and provides early training detached from industrial pressures.

The **West German** approach is not dissimilar. From the age of twelve, students in the secondary modern school follow a compulsory course in work studies – technical skills and working methods. In the intermediate school and *Gymnasium* the course is still compulsory but forms part of social studies and natural science. Education from 15–18, either full or part-time, is compulsory. Twenty-five per cent of the age group continue on full-time upper secondary courses in the *Gymnasium* leading mainly to the *Abitur*, although the point was frequently stressed that, increasingly, the *Gymnasium* has come to satisfy the needs of young people who are not seeking university entrance but require high basic standards for training as speech therapists, computer programmers, and the like. Eleven per cent of the age group enter full-time vocational training in technical and trade schools whilst an impressive 64 per cent join what is called the 'dual' system, through 1.7 million apprenticeships. It is in this field of post-15 vocational training that West Germany's excellence would be hard to match. Altogether, there are 460 recognised occupations for which practical occupational training takes place mainly on the job, with eight–twelve hours weekly in vocational schools – 60 per cent on trade training and 40 per cent on general education. Skills to be acquired are all precisely defined in occupational training regulations. Training is subject to a formal contract in 'training firms' specially designated by the Country's 116 Chambers of Trade and Industry, and trainees receive progressive rates of pay related to stage of training, occupation and area.

Retention in the system at 95 per cent is phenomenally high. Two over-riding virtues of dual training are claimed: employers tend to respond more rapidly to technological change than do schools and colleges; and training on the job is largely practical and so prospects are better for coordinating training and employment. Those leavers not absorbed into the dual system can opt at 15 for a one-year introductory course, of which there are two types – the basic vocational training year and the occupational preparation year.

Systems in **Sweden** are strikingly different. Education to 16 is strictly non-vocational. Throughout the compulsory comprehensive school the accent is on a broadly-based common course. Mixed-ability teaching is the rule: streaming and setting are forbidden: homework is only occasional, and leaving examinations do not exist. For the last year of compulsory schooling, two experimental introductory vocational courses were introduced in 1980 – a four-week study programme providing an introduction to upper secondary courses; and a 40-week job introduction course mounted by the upper secondary school in collaboration with employers. As in Denmark, early leaving arrangements exist for the school-tired 15-plus who can transfer to an adjusted course of study consisting of five hours weekly in school and the balance with an employer. At 16-plus, no less than 85 per cent of leavers enrol in the integrated upper secondary school which brings together under one roof the former academic upper secondary school and various other forms of education and training. With this type of school Sweden has probably gone further than any other country towards the successful integration of all 16–19 provision. Places are, incidentally, available for the whole age group. Twenty-five 'lines' of study, two, three or four years in length, are grouped broadly in three sectors – arts and social; economics and commercial; and scientific and technical. Strict weekly timetabling across the country is imposed through a national curriculum. Approaching half the enrolments are in two-year vocational lines and more than one-third are in the longer, theoretical lines such as natural sciences and technology.

Besides these formal lines of study, a comprehensive range of 450 specialised courses is offered, mainly vocational and lasting from one week to five years. From what I saw and was told, the system clearly works well. Integration of all 16–19 provision has four aims: a broadening of the curriculum; ease of transfer between courses; deferment of career choice; and the blurring of the distinction between education and training. What this means in timetable terms is illustrated by the following example: out of a working week of 38 hours in the two-year workshop technical line, one hour is allocated to labour market orientation, three hours to one or more of ten 'liberal' options, two hours to physical education, four hours in the first year only to Swedish, and 32 hours to workshop technology.

Of the remaining leavers, eight per cent enter traditional apprenticeships and three per cent go directly into work. Links between school and working life are fostered in an admirably practical way by local planning councils (SSA Councils) on which schools, employers, unions, and the employment service are represented. Councils coordinate work experience and study visits, monitor local employment opportunities, and mount courses and conferences for staffs. A Youth Guarantee has operated since 1980, vesting responsibility for all under-18s in the education service.

Wide choice of study routes is the outstanding feature of the **French** system. From the age of eleven or twelve all children attend the comprehensive school (*collège unique*) and usually at 14 either continue in the same school for their fourth and third classes (85 per cent) or transfer to the vocational *lycée* (*lycee d'enseignement professionnel*) (12 per cent). Those who stay in the *collège* all follow a compulsory course of one and a half hours weekly (in each year) of manual and technical education, and may choose one of three technology options – industrial, economic and manufacturing. I found of particular interest the facility for pupils to transfer at this comparatively early age to the vocational *lycée* for three-year courses leading to a trade qualification. A comprehensive range of 300 subjects is offered and, of a long working week of 36 hours, half is timetabled for general education courses and half for vocational and technical training, including attachments to firms. Besides these two large groups of students, other smaller groups go directly into apprenticeships (0.5 per cent) and three types of pre-vocational courses.

The second cycle of secondary education begins at 15-plus and three study routes are available. Fifty-three per cent of the age group enrol at the traditional *lycée* and the expanding general and technical *lycée* (*lycée d'enseignement général et technologique*) – the combined former academic and technical *lycées* – for three-year 'long' courses. Half the enrolments are for the *baccalauréat* which is both school leaving examination and automatic passport to higher education. Half are for the *baccalauréat de technicien* which is available in 16 options grouped broadly into industrial and applied sciences, business and commercial studies, information science, and music. Standards in both *baccalauréats* are impressive – a national pass-rate of 64 per cent in 1980 – and it was humbling to see in both Rennes and Lille the facilities in *lycées* for applied science, the obvious commitment of staff and students and, not least, the working day of 8 am to 6.15 pm. Some students in the *lycée* proceed to the more narrowly vocational *brevet de technicien*. These three-year courses show greater technical and industrial bias, and the 57 different *brevets* are grouped in twelve broad types such as textiles, glass and building. Twenty-three per cent of the age group join the vocational *lycée* for the two-year 'short' courses leading to a craft qualification, the *brevet d'études professionnelles*. Sixty-two types of course are mounted and the main emphasis is on group work in well equipped workshops and on carefully graded and monitored industrial attachments. For nearly a quarter of French school leavers this represents a valuable contribution to the transition from school to work.

Something over six per cent of the age group enter two-year apprenticeships in a wide range of trades with part-time attendance at an apprentice training centre. The apprentice contract is admirably clear in its requirement for a properly trained and experienced craftsman to oversee practical training in the work place. Payments to apprentices are progressive, rising from 15 per cent of national minimum rates at the beginning of the contract to 45 per cent at the end. Two taxes on training are applied in France: the first, 1.1 per cent of payroll in firms employing more than ten employees, finances ongoing training; the second, 0.5 per cent of payroll, finances apprenticeships. Adult education, mounted by the Ministries of Education and

Labour, continues as a major contributor to vocational training and re-training. A national agency for *éducation permanente* was established in 1973 and upwards of one and a half million workers participate annually.

Work experience and guidance

Work experience in its various forms is widely practised in all four countries. In West Germany it is particularly well structured with preparatory work and three weeks in a firm, followed by de-briefing. In Sweden, the extent of highly integrated work experience for 14–15 year olds was increased from three to six weeks annually in 1982 with a long-term objective of ten weeks. Arrangements for teacher industrial attachments are interesting. In the integrated upper secondary school, post-16 work experience takes the form of an eight-week course – Course of Study and Working Life – which comprises study visits and carefully supervised practical experience in work places. In France, vocational courses commonly incorporate industrial observation and attachment, and the two-year craft courses in the vocational *lycée* are notable for the quality of their industrial placements.

Careers education and guidance services are well developed in all four countries and each has some particular merit. Although there is division of responsibility for the careers service in Denmark, some careers counsellors share their time between a consultancy role for careers teachers in schools and work in labour exchanges. One important strength of the system is that there is an automatic annual check on the progress of each school leaver for two years after leaving. In the upper secondary school, up to 20 periods in the gymnasium course are allocated to careers education, and school counsellors usually accompany the same group through their three-year course. Vocational counselling starts early in West German secondary schools. Occupational counselling and placement are the responsibility of the Federal Government through a growing network of superlatively provisioned counselling centres, a fine example of which I visited in Düsseldorf. There is, however, no on-going monitoring. The existence of the Youth Guarantee in Sweden has significant implications for the careers service. The service is staffed by careers teachers and non-teaching vocational consultants, with widespread support from the imaginative application of computer techniques. Careers guidance in France is particularly noteworthy. It is structured at three levels. In each establishment, there is a well-provided information centre and an action team responsible, *inter alia*, for mounting careers seminars, visits and the like. At district level, the educational and careers guidance centre is the base for an extremely thorough and on-going course and vocational guidance service with highly formal reviews at the end of the fifth and third classes. Nationally, through regional offices, the National Information Service on Teaching and Careers issues pamphlets and parents' handbooks of striking quality and attractiveness.

Special measures for the young unemployed

Only Denmark and Sweden operate schemes broadly similar to the Youth Training Scheme in Britain. All four countries concentrate their main efforts on intensive counselling and directing back into full or part-time education and training those young people who leave school at the earliest opportunity and who are without work or completed vocational training. Compulsory national service – armed forces, police and community service – continues to apply in each country, lasting between nine and twenty-two months.

Unemployment in the 16–25 age group in Denmark exceeded 17 per cent in 1983, and the ratio of youth to overall unemployment was put at 2:1. The Danes have long recognised that the most vulnerable young people are those who leave school at 15 or 16, having rejected traditional education and training, and it was with their needs particularly in mind that a number of initiatives were introduced in 1982. These culminated in the introduction of a Youth Guarantee in 1983 which is aimed to guarantee every young person an offer of either education or training, or employment. What was known as the 1982 'March package' included: measures to strengthen education/training provision through the development of basic and adult vocational training and more attractive opportunities for 16 year olds; the establishment of a compulsory municipal youth guidance service charged with monitoring every school leaver until 19 at least; adding 5,000 places to the EFG Basic Vocational Scheme; and creating apprenticeships and training places in the private sector through a subsidy scheme giving 30,000 Danish kr (£2,100) for every new place 'above the average for the last two years, less one', and in the public sector (5,000 more places). More radical by far than these, however, was the 1982 Job Creation Act which diverts funds from unemployment payments to creating new jobs which must in some way benefit the community. Urban renovation, re-cycling of materials and alternative forms of energy are examples. The Youth Guarantee works in three phases. Initially there is the counselling phase in which the unemployed young person is intensively counselled with a view to enrolling on a course or one of the special measures. Then comes the combined-offer phase, for a minimum of nine months, starting with an offer of training or education within trades, matching as far as possible the young person's preference, possibly leading to a longer course or, in the event of a shorter course, supplemented by another course or short-term employment. Last of all there is the final-offer phase (in the event of failure of the combined-offer phase) under which the young person must be offered a job for a minimum of nine months at the appropriate wage rate, supplemented by grants in some circumstances, such as a girl employed in a traditionally male occupation. In this final phase every effort is made to see that offers enhance prospects for permanent employment. In cases where a job in the private sector is unavailable, an opportunity must be created by the municipality.

The Directorate of Adult Vocational Education has introduced a six to eight week work introduction course, attached to the equivalent of our skills centre, expressly to relieve youth unemployment. This aims to give an introduction to several skills and trades. Although somewhat superficial, this course is apparently successful at achieving permanent employment. Variable employment subsidies, paid since 1978 to employers prepared to take on young people unemployed for three months, account for only five per cent of participants in special programmes, but their employment success rate, too, is high at 75 per cent.

It is a measure of West German achievement that youth unemployment was no higher than seven per cent in 1983 and this level was, moreover, close to the adult rate. Comparatively little use is made of conventional job creation measures. Compulsory education or training to 18, either full or part-time, aims at reducing the number of young people joining the labour force direct from school. To this end, the optional tenth year in the secondary modern school is currently the subject of fierce political debate: if it were a compulsory year, 330,000 training places in firms would be saved. A programme of priorities was drawn up in 1979 for the years up to 1982, providing for the accelerated implementation of the year of basic vocational training with a target of 90,000 places by 1982, the establishment of courses for secondary modern school failures, a progressive increase in the number of training places in firms, and the expansion of local workshop centres and vocational schools.

A significant feature of the West German system is 'polyvalence' – a broadly based vocational training to allow changes of job and preserve flexibility. One form of job creation is practised, under which the young worker is employed with a normal labour contract at standard pay rates for a fixed period not exceeding six months, renewable for a further six. Work is in teams under a qualified supervisor. A recent assessment shows that net job cost is low because of savings in unemployment benefit, and the project itself generates jobs in firms supplying goods and services for it. Other measures in the Federal Republic include short-time working with up to 68 per cent of lost wages made up by the State, the compulsory training levy on firms failing to respond to the call for more training places, and the trend towards a shorter working week (about one per cent reduction per year).

With 16–19 unemployment still at a modest 8.7 per cent in 1983, the measures devised by the Swedish authorities are designed to cope with relatively low numbers of young people, most of whom suffer from social, learning or emotional handicaps. A special Commission on Employment has strongly recommended a combined labour market/education approach: 'Society must guarantee all young people education, practical experience or work'.[2] Consistent with this over-riding objective, since July 1980 all under-18s have been the respon-sibility of the education service. Vocational guidance officers, supported by SSA Councils, go to extraordinary lengths to monitor, advise and generally nurture the Swedish 'rest' group and to keep contact with every individual young person. Those who are neither in satisfactory employment nor attending upper secondary courses are encouraged to enrol on short, work-orientated courses such as the eight-week course – Study Routes and Working Life – in the upper secondary school which is directed primarily at the young unemployed who remain undecided about a choice of career and who are unable to gain admission to the course of their choice. Other short courses are the four and 40-week courses offering educational and vocational induction programmes.

The Swedes acknowledge the merits of a break at 16-plus. It is a widespread practice to take a year off and enrol in upper secondary a year later. Municipal work schemes are imaginative and excellently tailored to suit local circumstances, and all have a marked training bias. In Uppsala, ten per cent of the cohort (200 young people at any time) are in the care of five counsellors in one or more of four progressive stages: four residential places provide basic skill training and are staffed on a one-to-one ratio; a workshop with twelve places and three staff provides skill training in joinery, cookery and housekeeping, and attracts a £5 daily allowance; 40 places for trade skills use intensive 'father figure' support and attract unemployment benefit of £6.70 daily; and there are 40 placements in firms with less intensive support and which attract the rate for the job. In Gothenburg, I visited the impressive Youth Centre West. Housed in a former army officers' mess, this serves as a drop-in centre for about 500 of the 2,000 young unemployed in the city. Over-20s qualify for labour market training under the Labour Market Board which attracts carefully graded daily and special incentive allowances.

No fewer than 750,000 of France's two million unemployed in April 1983 were in the 16–24 age group. Youth unemployment is more serious among girls because 300,000 young men are serving their year's national service at any time. The Mitterand Government reviewed the situation on coming to office and adopted a fresh approach, called the *Plan Avenir Jeunes* (Youth Plan). Special programmes designed to occupy the unemployed do not exist. Instead, two kinds of scheme operate in France – subsidised jobs and training initiatives. There are two employers' incentive measures. The first, offering 280,000 places, allows employers a 50 per cent remission of social security charges on condition that their labour force in one year exceeds that of a year before. Priority groups for this concession are young people who completed vocational training or national service up to two years before, and widows and single parents of up to ten years standing. The second, offering 125,000 places, gives total remission of all social security charges to firms defined as *entreprises artisanales* of up to ten employees taking on an apprentice and partial remission to firms with more than ten employees. There are six schemes to provide the young unemployed with basic vocational training. Four of these are particularly interesting. The vocational attachment (*contrat emploi-adaptation*) in a firm for 16 year olds (with completed training) or 18 to 26s lasts for six months and must include a minimum of 150 hours' training in a firm or training establishment. Pay is at 90 per cent of the minimum rate and is met by the State. The Employment with Training Contract (*contrat emploi-formation*) for 16 year olds (qualified) or 17 to 26s amounts to a contract of at least one year with 200–500 hours' vocational training, or two years with 500–1200 hours' training. The rate for the job is paid, including training time. The preparatory vocational attachment (*contrat emploi-orientation*) for the 16–26s offers options which last from five to eight months to allow untrained young people to sample a trade and up to one year to give an opportunity for full or partial vocational training. Up to 18 years of age, 25 per cent of the minimum rate is paid, with boarding and transport allowances. From 18–26, 75 per cent of the rate is paid. Finally, there is the formal apprenticeship mentioned earlier. Seventy-nine per cent of the young unemployed had been absorbed in these schemes by June 1983.

The employers' view

Employers' criticisms generally of the education service in Denmark, West Germany and Sweden had a familiar ring. The order varied, but in all three countries school leavers' standards in their own language (spoken and written), the practical application to working life of basic mathematical processes, and young people's attitudes to working life were criticised. Danish employers consider a staying-on rate of nearly 40 per cent to the academic *gymnasium* too high. They feel it produces a disproportionate loss to industry of the most able, and would prefer the introduction of admission limits. Large employers, particularly, commend the basic vocational education programme (EFG), and work experience is supported widely, although the conditions for it could be improved and extended. They reject all special measures for the young unemployed where these offer no training component or long-term prospect. West German employers are strongly critical of what they regard as the high failure rate of twelve per cent in the secondary modern school. They, too, are unhappy with the proportion of young people transferring to the academic *Gymnasium* and university entrance at a time when technological change calls for a constant supply of skilled technicians and craftsmen. The 'dual' system of vocational training and the basic vocation education year are both highly regarded. Although Swedish employers are of the view that their workers were better trained when industry itself was responsible for training, they recognise that conditions have changed since the days of traditional apprenticeships and now accept the strengths of the integrated upper secondary school, with its broader training base and deferred career choice. The Employers Confederation is impressive in its supportive attitude both to education and training and to work experience. The notion of the Creative School – 'everybody can be successful at something; stimulation follows from the feedback of results'[3] – I found unusually interesting.

The response of French employers was different. No criticisms of basic standards emerged – probably the product of a good general education pursued throughout vocational and non-vocational courses alike. In quantitative terms, employers insist that too many young people are being trained for the clothing industry (suffering from foreign imports) and for the tertiary (that is, service) sector with the exception of higher level courses in the technical *lycée*; there is apparently a national shortage of top level technicians. In qualitative terms, there is dissatisfaction with the quality of craftsmen trained on the three-year vocational *lycée* course starting at 14-plus. Wastage rates are high and it is said that training often lacks relevance. Employers' preference for apprenticeships with attendance at apprentice training centres and for two-year courses at the vocational *lycée* is marked.

The impression given to parents and the public in Britain must be that, with a succession of reports on 16–19 provision, our national plan is definitively laid. The European experience shows how deficient we are. Indeed, the truth is that our re-thinking has only just begun.

Lessons for the United Kingdom

My report identifies a number of lessons for the 14–19 age group in Britain. Most, needless to say, have financial implications. Some may be seen as controversial. I deal first with the question of preparation for greater leisure and long-term unemployment.

Although all four countries I visited – Denmark, France, Sweden and West Germany – recognise the need to prepare young people for leisure by the time they leave school, none has taken any particularly radical measures to deal with it in schools. Throughout, 14–16 year olds are, however, offered a somewhat broader diet of optional and compulsory courses in handicrafts, music, photography, art, team sports, motor knowledge and the like than in Britain. But the serious criticism which emerged more than once was that the formalisation of leisure may serve to encourage young people to participate in uniform, recognised activities rather than to explore the wealth of alternative uses of leisure. The range of timetabled leisure pursuits offered to young Swedes is wider than I saw elsewhere, and in France the ten per cent of school hours which can be allocated to grant-aided educational projects of all kinds allows unusual scope for developing leisure-type activities off the school premises.

Against this background of European experience, early consideration could usefully be given here at national level – possibly in the context of responses to DES Circulars 6/81 and 8/83 (*The School Curriculum*)[4] due in April 1984 – to the preparation for leisure content of the secondary curriculum for 14–16s. Besides an introduction to life-long pastimes, the development of individual as well as team sports, and personal enrichment, a great deal of inventive thought still needs to be applied to the changing nature and scope of leisure. For post-16 students, too, we have something to learn from Europe. In terms of school curriculum, the developing all-day comprehensive schools in some West German States offer an impressive range of afternoon activities with long-term leisure value which serves well as a model. In Sweden, provision for the development of physical education and sports in all their forms is particularly noteworthy, while the French require all post-15 students to follow courses of physical activity and offer imaginative options in what are called the 'plastic arts'.

We in Britain need urgently to look more constructively at curricular developments in all post-16 provision, recognising the needs of greater leisure. Perhaps the time is right for a second curriculum document on the post-16 curriculum.

But it is in the area of adult education that we are most deficient. Denmark and Sweden shame us with their heavily subsidised youth schools, folk high schools and study circles offering maximum flexibility of timing, range of activities and client group. Even paid leave of absence is available. The Federal Republic is no less successful with the adult education college and a wealth of voluntary provision, including facilities widely provided by employers. France has gone a good deal further than Britain with university involvement in adult education, while the Université du Troisième Age is expanding its activities from the elderly to all age groups. Unlike adult education in Britain, *éducation permanente* in France is alive and well.

What is the message for ourselves? Local education authorities have a duty to provide for leisure time occupation for those over compulsory age. In practice, the Russell Report's[5] recommendation of two per cent of an authority's education expenditure to be allocated to adult education has never been achieved. Indeed, the trend has been quite the reverse. Adult education is progressively less subsidised, and a nationally shrinking service now attracts little more than five per cent of post 16-year olds. The regeneration of adult education, both local authority and voluntary, is overdue, allied with a widening of its scope and purpose. Leisure, both voluntary and enforced, will increase, and adult education is an important agency in filling the gap. Its therapeutic value should not be dismissed; nor should its important contribution to community life. Funding calls for a searching investigation into alternatives practised in Europe, such as payroll taxes. Paid leave of absence to attend approved non-vocational adult education programmes merits consideration if early retirement and other devices for reducing the labour force are to attract support.

Preparation for working life

14–16 age group

Set beside these four European countries, Britain is still experimenting uncertainly with the preparation for working life of the 14–19 age group. True, there is a sharp division of practice between the four over the vocational content of the curriculum for 14–16 year olds, but there are lessons to be learned all the same. Work experience in the last two years of compulsory education appears better practised in all four countries than in Britain. The Danes stress its value as a means of choosing work rather than introducing young people to the conditions for it. In West Germany, work experience for all 14 and 15 year olds (with the exception of *Gymnasium* students) is particularly well structured. Great emphasis is placed in Sweden on the integration of work experience into school work, and pupils in their last two years of compulsory schooling are required to undertake a minimum of one week annually of three broad areas: technical/manufacturing, commercial, social. The French are, admittedly, more selective, with work experience forming an integral part of vocational courses, but attachments are well planned and monitored.

As with preparation for leisure, the opportunity should not be missed in this country to review the vocational content of the curriculum for 14–16s as an essential ingredient of the development of curriculum policies set in motion by the Secretary of State in 1981. The draft circular asks, amongst other things, for details of the steps taken to ensure the curriculum is balanced, coherent, suited to pupils across the full ability range, related to what happens outside school, and that it includes sufficient applied and practical work. The balance is a fine one. Too many computer programmers trained too late, or training in technologies which are already defunct, represent a serious disservice to young people. Up to 16-plus a more imaginative, broadly based, integrated approach, incorporating compulsory pre-vocational courses and relevant work experience is surely the only sensible goal. There is, of course, no single answer for all our schools. Local initiatives cannot be displaced by central direction. Central direction might work successfully in Europe but I cannot see the traditional autonomy of local education authorities in Britain being readily abandoned. It is healthy that distinctive schemes such as the Schools Council Industry Project, Understanding British Industry, and Opening Windows on Engineering, together with other national and local initiatives, should be encouraged in their different ways.

Despite misgivings, most local education authorities displayed an active interest in the Manpower Services Commission's Technical and Vocational Education Initiative (TVEI). Admittedly, for many, it was a question of gift horses. Whilst it is true that, in general, the fourteen pilot schemes started in the Autumn Term of 1983 compare unfavourably with the French vocational *lycée* with its three-year course spanning the 14–17 age groups, a start has been made. Fifty to sixty extra schemes are now going to be funded from September 1984. But what is disappointing is that, even with these, only two per cent of the secondary school population will be participating (compared with twelve per cent in France).

It is premature to judge the long-term curricular benefits of TVEI. Much will depend on its attraction beyond 16. At the risk of causing widespread offence, I cannot resist questioning the whole morality of investing £0.4 million annually in 250–1,000 pupils – a unit cost of £400–£1,600 each – when the same money could have been used to better effect for a much bigger group of all abilities, still enhancing technical and vocational education in schools, simply by allocating the funds to individual authorities to be used at their discretion. The 14–18 schemes may well be appropriate for some, but 14–16 schemes could prove to have wider appeal. Flexibility could be preserved, and the need for long term commitment to the Scheme at 14 avoided. But, having said all that, TVEI is a reality and the opportunity to tap the £20 million annually cannot logically be missed by any local authority.

There is wide diversity of practice in Europe for recording pupil achievement. Sweden has virtually abandoned formal examinations; France is the most certificated of all. But both, with Denmark and the Federal Republic, have adopted pupil profiling systems of different forms which enjoy credibility among employers and clearly influence the preparation for work in schools. The draft policy statement on Records of Achievement for School Leavers, with its proposals for pilot schemes, published in November 1983, is therefore to be welcomed. The City and Guilds system pioneered with YOP in mind and covering 14 basic abilities is one useful model but there are others, such as the Swindon Scheme, while the Further Education Unit[6] stresses that the profile is 'right at the heart of learning'. It is not designed as a supplement to other means of assessment. If the intention is that it is for public consumption then it must form an integral part of certification.

It is too early to predict the success of the Government's School Curriculum Development Council in reshaping the preparation for working life curriculum for 14–16s. European practices show that there is much to be done.

16–19 age group

For 16–19 year olds in Britain the prospectus of routes to working life bears all the hallmarks of crisis planning. Whilst I concede that sharply rising youth unemployment demanded prompt action, we have been stampeded into policies and structures which could well fail the needs of young people in the longer term. Faced similarly with rising unemployment, all four of our European neighbours have stuck resolutely to policies which reflect traditional practices and exploit facilities already well established. Denmark and the Federal Republic settled on mainly employer-based training, Sweden and France on education-based programmes. We in Britain faltered in not making up our minds on this point. The result is confusion of responsibility and, what I suspect, an expensive coordinating role for the Manpower Services Commission in conducting a scratch orchestra of players offering further education provision, employer-based training and freelance training agencies.

Approaching 50 per cent of young Danes join the three-year basic vocational education programme at 16, structured on a system of boards for each broad vocational area which are in the hands of employers and unions. The Federal Republic does even better. Two-thirds of German leavers at 15 enter the 'dual' system of training. Sweden, with its impressive integrated upper secondary school (attracting 82 per cent of leavers), and France with its vocational *lycée* (twelve per cent) and the expanding general and technical *lycée*

(53 per cent), have opted for provision based on their education services.

Integrated provision

My argument is that thinking in Britain is muddled. We have a hybrid of further education, employer-based training and, latterly, MSC-sponsored programmes. The mix is tricky and expensive to coordinate satisfactorily; regional planning is complicated; there is risk of duplication and waste of resources; and standards are hard to monitor and guarantee. My view, and it is a personal one, is that an integrated education/training approach within the education service would have offered better promise. Coinciding with sharply declining secondary rolls, accommodation for the first time in memory would have been available for expansion of wide ranging post-16 (or post-14) opportunities on Swedish/French lines. But the die is cast, and I must dwell on lessons to be learned for the structure we now have.

In curricular terms, Europe has much to teach us in providing for 16–19s. The youth school in Denmark is an important provider of basic vocational courses and the first year of the basic vocational education programme (EFG) requires participants to select one of eight broadly based vocational areas, apportioning time between vocational studies (60 per cent) and general studies (40 per cent). In the Federal Republic, the eight to twelve hours weekly spent in vocational schools by students in the dual system is similarly shared 60 per cent on trade training and 40 per cent on general education. Centralist control in Sweden prescribes weekly timetabling in the integrated upper secondary school and facilitates maximum ease of transfer between courses and disciplines. Apart from the major vocational component of the 'lines' of study (30 hours out of 38 hours weekly), all students follow a one-hour course of orientation on the labour market and the balance of time on courses in physical education, Swedish and a list of option subjects which include other languages and consumer education. Choice of study routes is the keynote of the French system. Long, three-year courses are offered in *lycées* leading either to the demanding and prestigious general *baccalauréat* (now including agricultural science and technology) or to the technical *baccalauréat*. Short, two-year craft courses are mounted in the vocational *lycée* with a marked emphasis on technical and trade training and industrial attachments (22 hours out of 36).

The most important message for Britain from all this is the overwhelming case for 'polyvalence'. This is a broad, basic vocational training up to 18 or 19, improving the prospects for movement to reflect the changing nature of employment, and deferring career choice to the latest possible. True, progress has been made in Britain with the *Basis for Choice* (ABC) programme for uncommitted students at 17-plus, and the Joint Working Party Report, *ABC in Action*[7] underlines the new flexibility of approach expected of teachers working in this field and the importance of profiling. Equally, the Certificate of Pre-Vocational Education[8] being progressively developed through City and Guilds submissions in some local education authorities is a move in the right direction, particularly for those young people who feel the Youth Training Scheme is inappropriate to their needs. The 60 per cent common core with practical work in one of three options, attachment to a local employer, and careers guidance has considerable promise, so long as the criteria and syllabuses are put into practice by schools and colleges.

On the timing of entry into further education, the Swedes particularly acknowledge the advantage of a break from school at 16. It is widespread practice for young Swedes to take a year off with the intention of enrolling in the integrated upper secondary school a year later. To some undecided young people, this allows an opportunity to attend short work taster courses and pre-vocational programmes, and to sort out their ideas before embarking on full-time education.

The task is wider and infinitely more complicated, but the Secretary of State's review could profitably extend to the 16–19 curriculum in all its guises. There is merit even in applying the discipline of committing to paper what the education service hopes for this age group; what Youth Training Scheme initiatives plan to achieve in education and training terms; and how examination structures determine what is taught.

The contribution of adult education to post-16 vocational education and training in Europe is limited and even more limited in Britain. The Manpower Services Commission has published its discussion paper *Towards an Adult Training Strategy* but sensibly it recognises that the MSC cannot by itself develop a comprehensive adult training strategy[9]. The Commission expects to exercise more the role of a catalyst but, as usual, much will depend on funding and local participation.

Education and training

The approach in all four countries to the government and management of education and training is fundamentally different from our own. In Denmark, responsibility for education lies with the Ministry of Education, organised in five directorates, three of which are for upper secondary, vocational, and further and higher education respectively. Control is through regulations, allocation of funds, issue of guidelines and curriculum development. In the Federal Republic, responsibility for education, including vocational schools, is devolved to the Länder whereas Federal powers extend to non-school vocational training and further training. There is, however, close and increasing collaboration between the Federal and Länder authorities on vocational training and the expansion and improvement of further education. There is also a large measure of coordination through the Conference of Ministers of Education and the Federal–Länder Commission for Education Planning. Sweden has probably gone further than any other country towards blurring the distinction between education and training. The National Board of Education administers all forms of education and training, including adult, and controls budgets, curricula, in-service training and research. The French system is not dissimilar. Two Ministries – Education and the Universities – administer the whole state system. With the few exceptions of some vocational education which is controlled by other ministries such as Agriculture, the Ministry of Education exercises responsibility for all education and training through nine directorates and 25 geographical *académies*. Two advisory councils, one covering technical education, complete a thoroughly integrated structure of administration.

Based on successful European practice, urgent consideration should be given to the title and role of the Department of Education and Science. The DES could be retitled the Department of Education and Training (DET) and its role revised correspondingly to complement that of the Department of Employment. Certainly, the prospects for a more consistent and equitable provision of education and training for working life would be better with single direction at government level. Education and training services should be one entity and the MSC brought into the educational partnership. A new Department of State could embrace education and training for 14–19 year olds, and a comprehensive curriculum could be devised for the whole age group, either full or part-time. An imposed tertiary system is probably unrealistic, but it is surely not unreasonable to ask local education authorities and training agencies to lay coherent plans for the whole age group.

School leaving

With increasing numbers of leavers at 16-plus being recruited to Youth Training Scheme programmes, there could be a case for reconsidering school leaving rules. Indeed, many claim that the age is already being raised by stealth. Judging by trends in the four countries, staying-on rates in Britain are trailing by and large. In Denmark, with the 40 per cent enrolments in the upper secondary school and 42 per cent enrolments on the three-year Basic Vocational Education Programme, most young people continue in full-time education after 16. West Germany has formalised the position completely since 1969 with the requirement for full or part-time education to 18. At 15, 25 per cent proceed to *Gymnasium* studies, eleven to full-time vocational training and 64 per cent into the 'dual' system with its broadly based training. Sweden's impressive integrated upper secondary school absorbs 85 per cent of leavers at 16-plus, while eight per cent enter traditional apprenticeships and three per cent go directly into work. The record in France is broadly comparable: 53 per cent enrol at the traditional *lycée*, 23 per cent at the vocational *lycée*, and six per cent enter apprenticeships, while twelve per cent transfer to the vocational *lycée* at the earlier age of 14-plus. Staying-on rates across Britain are variable and there is a strong case for making education and training compulsory, either full or part-time, until 18. The West German view is that any training is better than none and I am inclined to another German doctrine that an adequate supply of trained labour can itself become an engine of economic growth.

Youth Guarantee

Whilst improved participation rates in education and training after 16 and YTS programmes have contributed to proper counselling and guidance during the early years after leaving school, we remain far short of our European neighbours in guaranteeing an effective service.

The Danes introduced a full Youth Guarantee in 1983 guaranteeing every young person an offer of either education or training, or employment, until 19. In the Federal Republic, compulsory full or part-time education or training to 18 has the same effect as a youth guarantee. The position in Sweden since 1980 has been clear: under the Youth Guarantee, all leavers at 16-plus who do not enrol in upper secondary are automatically the responsibility of the education service until their eighteenth birthday. Approaches in France are different but achieve the same objective. The Youth Plan (*Plan Avenir Jeunes*), introduced by the Mitterand Government, effectively guarantees either subsidised work or basic vocational training for those school leavers not enrolled on *lycée* courses or in apprenticeships. Against this background, European practices demonstrate the coherence and clear benefits of vesting responsibility for all young people to the age of 19 in the education service, whether in full or part-time educational training, in work, on YTS programmes, or unemployed. Monitoring of individuals is more easily facilitated and time-wasting duplication of records avoided. What is more, young people are already known to the education service and careers services, and their confidence in these services will sustain them through the difficult period after leaving school.

Careers

My impression is that all four countries treat careers education more seriously and thoroughly than we do in Britain. With typical German zeal, the Länder (States) provide vocational counselling (as opposed to occupational counselling) from the age of twelve or 14 on an impressive scale – aptitude testing, conferences for parents and pupils, psychological support and a technical advisory service on new technologies. Occupational counselling is the responsibility of the Federal Government. Swedish study and vocational orientation officers must all have had experience of working in industry, commerce or the public sector. Methods and materials are similar to those in Britain, but one criticism is that the service is largely used as an information service; little attempt is made actively to influence students. Job finding and placements are the responsibility of the National Labour Market Board, and model employment offices across the country are highly sophisticated in both equipment and function. Another practical feature of note of the Swedish system are the local planning councils, on which employment services are represented, which coordinate work experience placements and mount courses, conferences and work experience for careers teachers. France has the most structured information and careers guidance services of all. Throughout a pupil's school life regular meetings are held between teachers, guidance counsellors, doctor, psychologist and parents to provide vocational guidance, and at the end of the second and final years in the *collège* a proposed guidance programme is issued for each pupil which parents can either accept or appeal against. Given the duty placed on local education services to provide a careers service for persons attending full or part-time educational institutions (except universities) and to provide advice on suitable employment, assistance in obtaining employment, and to make the service available to university students who choose to use it, there are clear lessons for us in Europe. But fragmentation of responsibility for careers guidance and employment services has its risks. Some authorities have come perilously close to axing their careers services. Underspending on careers services has become common. And all this has taken place at a time when pressure on careers officers with Youth Training Scheme programmes, scarce employment and changing technologies is greater than ever before. For Britain, there is an unmistakable case for strengthening the careers service to meet the increased demands of both a youth guarantee and YTS initiatives. There is still some way to go in introducing computer techniques to careers guidance and job placement, and in relieving careers officers of administrative chores. Careers guidance procedures themselves call for a critical reappraisal to reflect the best in Europe, while careers literature, nationally published and funded, could well be modelled on the French.

Funding and student grants

Whilst it is true that we in Britain have experimented with ways of funding vocational training, particularly employer-based training, practices in Europe are variable but effective. I sense that they serve to fund state provision more realistically and motivate firms to achieve not only quality training but also cost effectiveness. In the Federal Republic, designation as a 'training firm' under the dual system is prized, and such firms commonly mount their own training schools. The funding of State-run vocational schools is shared between the Länder (for staffing) and local communities (for plant and equipment). The dual system requires nearly two million training places in firms, and the Training Places Promotion Act provides for a compulsory levy on firms not meeting their quota. The threat has not yet been applied. Swedish training is largely education provided, and grant aid to the National Board for job introduction courses based on upper secondary, and to firms and the National Board jointly for vocational courses in firms is on a strict place cost basis. In France, most vocational training is education-based but six per cent of leavers enter apprenticeships and a proportion enter specialist training establishments such as the Air France Apprentice School. Regardless of the nature of training, funding of vocational training after the third class is partly by way of a 1.1 per cent payroll training tax, and an apprenticeship tax of 0.5 per cent of the total wages bill on all employers who fail to provide their own initial training.

The scene in Britain is confused. With a mix of local education authority funded further education colleges, extremely variable employer provision, and the developing catalytic role of the Manpower Services Commission, the time is overdue for a fundamental review of funding post-16 (or post-14 in view of TVEI) vocational training. Payroll and apprenticeship taxes might well help to improve present uneven standards of training between industries and geographical areas. Duplication of, and gaps in, training are all too common. Any system that directs resources to where they are most needed and seeks to rationalise education funding can only be commended.

Denmark and West Germany have long accepted that the issue of post-16 study allowances is just as crucial as the quality and range of vocational training itself. The Danes have settled on an unpaid first year in their three year Basic Vocational Education Programme, followed by two years attracting apprentice or basic employee rates. The 64 per cent of West German leavers entering the dual system at 15-plus qualify for a 'salary' from the start of their three-year training which varies according to stage of training, trade and region, and is supplemented where the figure is unacceptably low. This has overtones of manpower planning, but from what I saw it is generally popular. Sweden has gone a good deal further and, up to 1980, paid to all young people at 16-plus attending the upper secondary school a wage of £350 monthly. This was controversially withdrawn and now the payment of £25 monthly approximates only to family allowance. In France, only the six per cent of young people at 16-plus who enter apprenticeships qualify for any special payment – rising from 15 per cent of minimum national rate for the job at the beginning, to 45 per cent at the end. Students at the various forms of *lycée* qualify only for the equivalent of family allowance.

All four countries acknowledge that the variable treatment of school leavers in grant terms is unsatisfactory. In Britain, the young unemployed tend to receive favourable treatment. Maybe they should. But the undoubted financial hardship to some families in supporting 16–19 education is well known. To allow decisions on study rates at 16-plus, either academic or vocational, to be determined largely by financial considerations, cannot serve the best interests of individuals or the nation. Progressive and variable student grants from 16–18 reflecting stage of course or training and other factors would serve to remove some, at least, of current inequalities, and facilitate a coherent training programme based more on training requirements and interests than on student financial support.

Adjusted courses and special measures

Denmark and Sweden have both accepted the merits of allowing school-tired adolescents to leave full-time academic education after the age of 14, subject to the offer of a trainee post or work, and attendance at a youth school. The task of operating the Youth Guarantee is complicated by this, but the general view is that the removal of young people in this group can only enhance the prospects of the remainder. Both West Germany (most States) and France have adopted systems that also allow departure from full-time schooling to vocational training before 16. Much of the undoubted success of the German structure is the result of sorting out problems at 15-plus. We should learn from these practices. Purists will insist on a broadly based, common core education to school leaving age. But it makes sense to have some form of adjusted course of study to enable, in approved cases, young people of 14-plus or 15-plus for whom further full-time school attendance is judged inappropriate, to attend full or part-time vocational courses, or to enter training contracts with approved employers.

Generally speaking, the main thrust of measures to relieve youth unemployment in all four countries is towards directing young people back into education or training and to creating subsidised jobs. It is true that special measures exist, but even with these, the emphasis is on new or improved training.

The main response to youth unemployment in Britain is the Youth Training Scheme for both employed and unemployed young people.

Reports suggest that uptake of places in the first year will be within 20 per cent of the 460,000 target envisaged, comprising Mode A (employer-based) and Mode B (college and training workshop based) schemes. It is tempting – and maybe too easy – to be critical of the whole philosophy of the scheme. Our European neighbours have resisted establishing any new management structure for provision for their young unemployed. Instead, their measures all rely on existing resources, whether education- or employer-based. We have settled on a hybrid path which adds to total costs, results in confusion and duplication of effort, and produces an uneven pattern across the country. In the event, of the 370,000 school leavers and 17 year olds on the Scheme, the majority – or more than 70 per cent – are receiving off-the-job training in colleges. This poses the question whether the Swedish and French models would have been more appropriate to Britain. In short, the Scheme could have been based on education and some, at least, of current worries about quality reduced. At the same time, one must recognise the difficulty of funding training from the £500 that remains after allowances of £1,350 have been paid from the £1,850 allowed by the Manpower Services Commission. An annual unit cost in further education of between £1,400 and £1,800 speaks for itself, and explains the regrettable reduction to thirteen weeks' training.

The single numerical target of the Youth Training Scheme in the first year of its operation was to offer suitable places for all unemployed 16 year-olds by Christmas 1983. In the event, this target was comfortably achieved. Commendation is also due to the MSC for the forward planning of its Training Division. The New Training Initiative (NTI) objectives have been positively and crisply identified: modernisation of skill training, quality monitoring, and access to training itself. One major deficiency of YTS as it currently operates is the absence for many young people of any link with further and improved qualification. It is clear that YTS risks being too independent. One of the many strengths of further education in this country is the ease of progression it offers: access is at any level and exodus at a point suiting the individual. Basically, YTS is only a start towards providing a fully integrated system of education, training and work experience for all young people to the age of 19. A second measure sponsored by the MSC is the Community Programme, the successor to the Special Temporary Employment Programme.

Schemes providing subsidies to employers taking on extra labour operate in all four countries and in Britain. A striking difference between the Young Workers' Scheme in this country and those else-where is the requirement for a training component on the Continent. Without exception, our European neighbours recognise that merely rewarding firms for increasing their labour force serves only to disguise problems and to postpone their surfacing. For those young people without vocational training, subsidy schemes in all four countries incorporate a compulsory training element, preparing young people for long term progression in work and the capacity to move between employers. The Department of Employment's Young Workers' Scheme, started in January 1982, is a measure designed specifically to relieve youth unemployment. The subsidy scheme is limited to those employers who pay wages of £45 or under to those under 18 who are in their first year of full time employment. Predictably, it has been criticised as an unsubtle device for depressing the wages of young people. There are currently 125,000 places, with no training component.

A great deal of scope remains in Britain for an expanded application of imaginative subsidy schemes, incorporating vocational training for those without such training or with incomplete training. Indeed, the growing view that the span of working life by the turn of the century will routinely involve two or three changes of occupation means that training and re-training will occur throughout life. Should this become a reality, then subsidised employment with an on-going training facility is likely to become commonplace.

Significantly, compulsory National – not exclusively military – Service in a variety of forms and of varying length still exists in all four countries – one year in France, nine months in Denmark, 15 months in the Federal Republic, and up to 22 months in Sweden. While this is not designed expressly as a measure to combat youth unemployment, the respective governments see such service partly as a means of securing a pool of trained military, police or community service personnel, and partly as a vehicle for training in practical and technical skills. Sensitive as the issue will be, a return to some form of National Service – armed forces, police and fire services, and community service – could be considered in this country. A shorter period of one year might be a compromise, with a strong training component for those without formal academic qualifications or vocational training.

Young people benefit indirectly from other broad-based measures for relieving unemployment in the four countries. In the Federal Republic, in particular, an impressive battery of measures has been employed for some years, including: short time working, under which 68 per cent of lost wages are made up by the State; shared working involving the sharing of one post between two employees; the trend towards a one per cent reduction yearly in the length of the working week; greatly expanded application of early retirement schemes; and a system of job substitution under which employees in senior positions reaching the final years of their working life are transferred to less senior positions but on protected salaries. The Federal Republic, too, is the only country of the four formally to raise its school leaving age to 18.

A great deal of scope remains in Britain for a closer examination of these and similar schemes.

References

1. National forum on education held at Bad Godesberg, quoted in *Education and Teaching in the Federal Republic of Germany* (Christoph Führ) 1979.
2. *The Employment Situation for Young Persons in Sweden*: National Board of Education (1980).
3. *Creative School Makes Transition into Working Life Easier*: Björn Grünewald (SAF) 1980.
4. Department of Education and Science Circulars: *The School Curriculum: Circulars 6/81 and 8/83.*
5. Russell Report (1973): *Adult Education - A Plan for Redevelopment.*
6. *Profiles*: Further Education Unit (1982).
7. *ABC In Action*: Further Education Unit (1982) - Department of Education and Science, London.
8. *17+: A New Qualification* (1982) - Department of Education and Science, London.
9. *The Shape of an Adult Training Strategy*: Manpower Services Commission (1983).

Acknowledgements

I should like to record my special thanks to John Banks at the Department of Education and Science International Division, and to my four programme coordinators: Paul Lyngbye in Copenhagen, Sabine Holzmann in Bonn, Kerstin Pehrsson in Stockholm, and Ives Bréard in Paris.

Finance for Education

My interest in the financial aspects of local government has grown in line with an increasing responsibility for budgetary matters in my own Authority. The scenario for finance in local government is currently in a state of flux, and I welcomed the chance the AEC Trust fellowship offered to take a critical look at alternative approaches to educational finance, and see how they function in the wider European context. Along with the personal stimulus my studies gave me, I hoped that, through the AEC Trust Fellowship, I might offer some useful contribution to the ongoing debate on local government finance in this country from a perspective that was specifically geared to education.

My journeys in Denmark have brought wider links between Denmark and West Glamorgan. Our Youth Orchestra/Choir has visited Arhus, and there are plans for the Youth Theatre Company to visit Roskilde. My hope is that these links will be extended in the future.

Clayton Heycock

Chapter 4   # Finance for Education

Clayton Heycock

Clayton Heycock, Deputy Director of Education for West Glamorgan, visited Italy, Norway, Denmark and Austria to study the very different approaches to the funding of compulsory schooling adopted in these four European countries. In analysing these financial systems he also looked at their effects on relationships between central and local government. He has been in his present post in West Glamorgan since 1974. Before that, he taught for six years in a large compre-hensive school, and spent a few years as a senior adviser with the former Glamorgan LEA. He has a degree in economics, and has masters degrees in education from each of the Universities of Leicester and Swansea.

The financial approaches to the funding of compulsory schooling within the European context are many and diverse. Current pre-occupations and present tensions in England and Wales may be under-stood better if they are compared and contrasted with those affecting some of our European neighbours. One of the chief difficulties here is selecting the most appropriate countries for critical appraisal. The most promising approach for this study was to explore in some depth specific facets of the financial systems working in Austria, Denmark, Italy and Norway. In this way, needless repetition could be avoided and the study could focus upon particular dimensions of relevance and importance to on-going dialogues in England and Wales. There were compelling reasons for choosing these four countries – and much to be learned from their experience.

The bulk of educational expenditure in any nation is likely to focus upon teachers' salaries. To this end, it was felt important to look at a country where such funding is centrally controlled. Italy was selected as it is highly centralised in its control of education and is a nation comparable in size and regional diversity to England and Wales. Consequently, it was hoped that some of the significant educational implications of centralised funding of teachers' salaries would become apparent.

In any detailed examination or evaluation of the current block grant funding approaches of central government in England and Wales, the very complexity of the calculations underpinning the distribution of such grant between local authorities, comes to the fore. It prompts the question: are there any simpler approaches in existence? The Norwegian experience, albeit in a much smaller nation, seems to have powerful and pertinent lessons in this respect, and is highlighted in this report. The more the current block grant mechanisms and approaches are analysed, the more the question of any alternative mode of funding by central government presents itself. Is the block grant unavoidable? Does any European nation look at its national funding role somewhat differently? The Austrian experience in the use of 'assigned revenues' for much of its regional and community funding is of particular relevance and offers a tested alternative to the block grant approaches. As such, it merits a full considera- tion.

To many, the debate regarding the future health of local govern- ment focuses upon an adequate local financial base and the accompanying and necessary autonomy in decision-making which comes in its wake. Is the rating system, as at present constituted, a sufficient source of localised funding? Do any of our European neighbours rely heavily on any alternative sources of local finance in their provision of services to their communities? Over a considerable period the Scandinavian nations have used local income tax as a vital source of finance for local government. Hence, it is important to look critically at the Danish experience and examine the limitations and potentialities of such an alternative source of local taxation. The following report offers some insights into alternative strategies to local government finance. Various approaches which deserve serious evaluation will be highlighted in the belief that we should avoid the dangerous conclusion that the only alternative approach for the future in England and Wales is to modify existing patterns. It may be that radical thought is overdue.

Funding of teachers' salaries: Italy

In Italy, pedagogically and financially, the education system spanning the compulsory years of schooling is highly centralised with the National Ministry of Public Instruction at the apex of the pattern of control. The examination orientated, highly regulation-conscious, educational provision is regarded very much as a State rather than a regional or community responsibility. The national government has through the years enacted a wider range of somewhat detailed legislative regulations (certainly by British standards) to govern the operation of the school system. These range from very explicit statements as to the maximum class size permissible in various types of school, to a detailed specification of the number of hours of instruction to be provided each week in various subjects at differing stages of education, and to a full elaboration of the conditions of service of teachers in different educational establishments. Overlaying this is a somewhat rigid bureaucratic interpretation of function within the National Ministry of Public Instruction and through its ninety or so provincial administrative offices. Largely for political reasons, there has been extreme reluctance to devolve responsibility for education to regional or local levels of government. Compared with a century ago, the involvement of local communities in the running of primary education is much more restricted.

The curriculum and the teaching profession are firmly the responsibility of the National Ministry. The funding of teachers' salaries is solely a State prerogative. Much of the rationale underpinning this centralised funding was that it would facilitate, at least initially, the objective of abolishing illiteracy and lead to equality of educational opportunity throughout the nation. Indeed, in most countries with a centralised specific grant type approach to the funding of much of educational expenditure, it is a concern to ensure minimum standards of provision throughout the country which is advanced as a major justification. Centralised funding of teachers' salaries in the Italian context has led to a buoyancy in teacher numbers and a significant improvement in pupil/teacher ratios (particularly in the primary sphere) in recent years. However, in any consideration of the distribution of teachers between areas and between schools, certain important features come to the fore.

Italy is essentially heterogeneous socially and culturally. The island communities of Sicily and Sardinia, each with its own distinctive ethos and background, are juxtaposed within the Italian State with regions bordering on Austria, Yugoslavia and France – each the subject of inter-country conflict at some stage, and each with a distinctive socio-linguistic cultural focus. The northern regions of Lombardy and

Piedmont, again each exhibiting a varied and distinctive historical base, are essentially different in orientation from the southerly regions straddling the cities of Naples and Bari. Seeing the contrast between life in Milan and life in Naples puts the situation into a contextual framework. Tuscany, focused on the architectural wonders of Florence, contrasts strongly with the Venetian culture stemming from the water engulfed City. To be fully aware of the heartbeat of Italy, it is vital to have an appreciation of the varied and extremely lengthy period of cultural diversity contained within the different parts of modern day Italy.

However, the major criteria for teacher apportionment are very much related to an acknowledgement of the sparcity factor as a major consideration and to a preoccupation with a maximum class size. Little or no recognition is given to a wide range of social and cultural characteristics within differing areas. The difficulties and complexities of evolving criteria to take account of such pertinent considerations in a large heterogeneous nation are forbidding. This is a problem inherent in any centralised evaluation of teacher needs. Allied to this, a further fundamental point which needs stressing (borne out not only in the Italian context but also in other countries such as Austria with centralised funding of teachers' salaries) is that it is almost inevitable that some regulations and guidelines underpinning the distribution of teachers will be needed. These will focus on qualitative evaluations with respect to such matters as class size, and will stem from a range of judgements on pedagogical matters. This process is likely to blur central and local government responsibilities within the curricular arena.

To expect to bring about such a major centralisation of educational funding in such a highly specific manner without an increase in regulatory control seems rather unrealistic. Such a process could alter, at the very least significantly and possibly fundamentally, the relative responsibilities of central and local government in the education sphere. It seems vital for all involved to appreciate these implications before embarking on what may seem, from some standpoints, to be an attractive funding reorientation. The 'local government' man, at least in his optimistic moments, will be wary of the possible loss of independence and decision-making. The more cynical administrator, tarnished by the difficulties and events of recent years, might feel that much of the so-called independence and autonomy is in any event illusory and the current financial pressures too burdensome to be allowed to continue.

Specific grant for education: Norway

Norway, with a land area which bears comparison with Italy and Britain, has less than one-tenth of the population of either country. Apart from a small number of cities (which are themselves small in European terms), the communities scattered throughout the nation are small. In such a situation, there is not the cultural and social variance found within the Italian or British scenarios. In the process of apportionment of resources, not least teacher expertise, the effects of sparcity dominate.

About one-half of the funding of compulsory schooling (spanning the ages of seven to sixteen) comes from a local income tax. The remaining monies come largely through a specific grant administered by the Ministry of Church and Education. The freedom accorded to local authorities in spending this money within the educational arena makes it similar in many respects to the suggested education block grant in England and Wales. The major objective of this Norwegian grant is to equalise disparities in the relative abilities of communities to fund education from their localised sources of finance, and thereby contribute to the achievement of equality of opportunity for all pupils. Perhaps its major significance lies in the simplified nature of the mechanisms underpinning this grant and the lessons for all involved in the planning of financial systems of whatever kind. As Kjell Eide, in his succinct account of this pattern of compulsory education financing in Norway stresses, highly complex systems may be anti-democratic:

> There is also an important relationship between the question of simplicity in instrument design and the aim of increased local and individual autonomy.. . . As an example, it could be mentioned that on the basis of detailed cost studies, we are in a position to design an extremely complex regression equation which could form the base for what would appear to be an absolutely 'fair' transfer system to the communes. It would take into account practically all involuntary variations in the costs of running local educational systems. The disadvantage, however, is that no one at the local political level or within schools would be able to figure out how the resulting figures were arrived at. They could not control whether they got the right amount, and they could not pick a fight on the question of whether the rules are the way they ought to be. As a consequence, we have deliberately abstained from this abstract form of 'justice', and we have strongly advocated a simple set of rules, easily understandable in its effect, and 'open' to criticism by those concerned for its various weaknesses.[1]

Eide's argument seems to highlight a common fallacy in public policy *vis-à-vis* financial instruments – namely that each individual instrument can be expected to fulfil the totality of policy objectives. In contradistinction at the heart of the Norwegian grant system are two fundamental concepts. Firstly, the notion of average teacher costs per '45-minute' period. This stems not from actual costs in a specific school but rather from assumptions about teachers' salary scales and average teacher–class contact throughout the country. Secondly, there is the notion of a percentage funding to individual local authorities linked to the fiscal capacity of a given area and, in particular, to average income *per capita*. To achieve the main aim of the grant, there are wide variations – from 25 to 85 per cent – in the percentage funding of average teacher costs as between local authorities. However, it is not with the objective of advocating the Norwegian system that these features have been highlighted here, but rather to stress the need for financial instruments to be readily understood by all those involved, particularly elected members and officers.

A further thought must be that the Norwegians, with a smaller population and far less social diversity, have seen fit to limit the objectives of their specific educational grant to equalising financial disparities between communities. Is it realistic in a larger and more diverse, national context to pin our faith in a complex 'Grant Related Expenditure' type of block grant approach in which the State arrogates to itself the ability to make detailed judgements on the localised expenditure needs of individual Authorities? How much more difficult, how much more fraught with the vicissitudes of apparent arbitrary weighting of factors, is such an all-embracing GRE type approach to the apportionment of educational expenditures. 'Let us remember the fundamental weaknesses of GRE assessments', Jack Springett has warned. 'They are based on assumptions about the needs of Authorities, and different assumptions (for example, about the needs of pupils with special educational requirements) could lead to quite different answers. A significant number of Authorities find the GRE levels of expenditure quite inadequate to meet their local needs.'[2]

A point of considerable significance, as a backcloth to the specific grant type approach in Norway, is the plethora of national regulations on such matters as school and class size. In essence, their effect is to place upon each local community a legal responsibility to ensure a minimum standard of resourcing and, in particular, a minimum level of teaching staff.

Assigned revenues: Austria

For nearly a thousand years Austria, and in particular Vienna, was at the heart of a much wider and larger Austro-Hungarian Empire. The nineteenth century witnessed very significant changes in the structure of this Empire and its death knell came in the wake of the First World War. For Austria, the next thirty years were to see two bloody wars, the first period of the Austrian Republic, and a long tortuous period of occupation of the country by foreign troops. The Post-1945 period has been a remarkable period of economic recovery, political stability and, in more recent years, of sustained economic growth labelled by many as the 'Austrian Economic Miracle'. To-day, Austria can boast a high standard of living for its population of some seven-and-a-half million inhabitants, a diversified economy continually updated and refined, and a wide range of services.

Austria is a federal republic comprising nine provinces. Parliament consists of a bicameral national assembly composed of a *Nationalrat* of 183 seats elected by all citizens over 19 under a system of proportional representation, and an Upper House, or *Bundesrat*, with fifty-three seats composed of representatives elected by each of nine provincial states in proportion to the population of each province. There is a provincial tier of government in each of the nine provinces elected by proportional representation of all citizens over 19 years of age. The regional government has administrative responsibility in certain spheres in which legislative responsibility remains with the national government, but in other spheres of activity it has legislative responsibility as well. The third tier of government in the Austrian context comprises some 2,300 local authorities or communities, of which over 2,000 have less than 5,000 inhabitants and only eight have populations in excess of 50,000. These authorities have no legislative powers and, as such, must function within the laws laid down by the *Bund* (national government) and the *Land* (provincial government). How does the system of compulsory schooling operate within this pattern of government? Under the 1962 constitutional law for the education system, educational policy making, save in a few special fields, was reserved to the Federal Government. At the same time, a distinctive role in school affairs was sought for the provinces and, to a lesser extent, the local communities. Pedagogical considerations are very much the concern and the responsibility of the Federal Government, and detailed guidance is given on such matters as the number of hours of study in each subject at each grade; the limits to be placed on class size in different schools; and the textbooks to be used within the various schools. Financially, teachers' salaries are a national government funding responsibility. Again, the various regulations, in large measure, ensure that the number of teachers employed in each area of the country in the differing schools are predetermined by national government edict.

The somewhat centralised pattern of control and the specific grant type funding of much of compulsory schooling is in contrast to the significant devolution of responsibility, at provincial and community levels, for most other services. It is the financial mechanism underpinning such extensive devolution of responsibility by the Federal Government which is of particular interest. At the heart of the financial approach to provincial-cum-municipality funding is a pattern of assignment of the revenues received nationally from a wide range of taxes. What are the essential features of this alternative strategy?

> An essential feature of the Austrian financial settlement is that the Federal Government, the *Lander* and the municipalities, are responsible for the outlay incurred in the discharge of their tasks. The actual allocation of financial resources is effected by means of what are known as "financial settlement laws", which are passed as simple federal laws. They are given concrete expression by political negotiations on the part of the area authorities.. . . The financial settlement laws, governing the allocation of resources, provide for comparatively longer time limits, at present, a six-year time limit.. . . The total yield of "joint Federal taxes" is allocated to the various levels of government on the basis of a division of revenue power . . . according to a formula determined collectively as part of the financial settlement negotiations.[3]

The assigned revenue approach seems important philosophically. Both central and local government come through discussion to evaluate how much revenue they require to provide their respective services and to agree how much of this revenue needs to be met from jointly assigned taxes. This appears to be very different in essence to a system whereby central government gives a grant to local government – a grant which seems susceptible to reallocation from time to time without much reference to service needs. Obviously, in reality it is possible for central government to dominate any joint discussions and, to an extent, this has happened in Austria.

One of the legitimate concerns of central government in its economic-cum-financial management role for the economy is the need to vary the emphasis, from time to time, on different kinds of taxation. It appears that a system of assigned revenues can span a sufficiently wide array of taxes to cohere with such state responsibilities. In other words, if the correct balance of assigned taxes is achieved, cyclical economic fluctuations can be met.

Pragmatically, a sharing of the nationally collected revenues of various forms of taxation does not have the problems of implementation associated with the introduction of many forms of local taxation. Consequently, it is a comparatively easy system to introduce. An important ingredient of the Austrian system is the longer duration of the financial settlement, spanning some six years. Clearly, a longer planning cycle is possible whatever the system – block grant or assigned revenues. The critical point is that in any reassessment of current financial practices, due weight and priority ought to be accorded to movement towards a longer financial settlement period.

Local income tax: Denmark

Over recent decades, a comprehensive pattern of social welfare provision has evolved in Denmark for citizens of all ages. The state has seen fit in an increasingly egalitarian society to develop one of the most extensive networks of social welfare to be seen in any nation. These developments have been accompanied by the decentralisation of responsibility to some 275 municipalities in a country of some five million inhabitants embracing a compact geographical area. Over the past couple of decades a further tier of local government – the fourteen counties – has evolved, with responsibilities for hospital provision and for post-compulsory and special education.

Compulsory schooling, spanning the ages of seven to sixteen years, is largely the responsibility of the municipalities. However, this responsibility operates within clearly defined regulations set by the National Ministry of Education. Guidelines are provided on such matters as class size and the minimum number of hours of tuition in various subjects. Indeed, the Ministry lays down in explicit terms at different ages the minimum and maximum number of hours of study within which each *Folkeskole* must operate. The Danish School Act 1976 states that:

> The aim of the *Folkeskole* is – in cooperation with parents – to give pupils a possibility of acquiring knowledge, skills, working methods, and ways of expressing themselves which will contribute to the all-round development of the individual pupil.

In all of its work, the *Folkeskole* must try to create possibilities of experience and self-expression which allow pupils to increase their desire to learn, expand their imagination and develop their ability for making independent assessments, evaluations and opinions.

The *Folkeskole* shall prepare pupils for taking an active interest in their environment and for participation in decision-making in a democratic society, and for sharing responsibility for the solution of common problems. The teaching and the entire daily life in school must be based on intellectual liberty and democracy.

The impact of the various regulations issued by the National Ministry of Education is to stipulate minimum levels of resourcing by each municipality within the sphere of compulsory schooling. Concurrent with the process of devolution of service responsibility at municipal level has come considerable freedom for local authorities in the financial arena. The monies received by local councils come partly from a block grant from national government. The amount of grant is based on a range of 'objective' criteria such as the number of miles of road, number of elderly persons, and number of children of compulsory school age. Other monies come from a tax on land and property, but there is tight state control on the maximum amount of income which can be obtained from such taxation. Above all else, the municipalities and counties receive monies from the levying of a local income tax. Indeed, it is not unusual for upwards of 75 per cent of the revenues of a municipality to emanate from a local income tax.

In Denmark, the local income tax is a flat-rate percentage tax, i.e. it is levied at the same percentage rate over the whole of an individual's taxable income. As such, it is somewhat regressive. At the same time it is partly ameliorated in the general income tax context because the state element of income tax is progressive in character. Each municipality is free to fix its own rate of local income tax, and this is fixed annually to the nearest tenth of a percentage point. Quite significant variations in the rates of local taxation occur between municipalities. Local income tax is collected simultaneously with the state income tax. It does not appear that the problems of assessment as between municipalities or the subsequent reimbursement of monies between the various tiers of government is too daunting. In this respect, it may be that some of the fears and forebodings regarding the practical difficulties (and, indeed, possible costs) of introducing a localised income tax in England and Wales have been exaggerated.

There are other implications for local government associated with using a local income tax as a central component in its financing system. The conflict between the financial autonomy of local government and the macro-economic management role of the state is much to the fore in any debate. Clearly perceptions will vary somewhat subjectively depending on the view taken of the role of government. Nevertheless, it is a fact that a pattern of localised income tax has formed the backbone of local government finance in the Scandinavian context for some years, and it has not led to irreconcilable conflicts between the needs of national and local government.

The income patterns in the Danish population exhibit less variation than in Britain. Consequently, the use of local income tax as a fund-raising mechanism does not require as much accompanying state funding to nullify or minimise differences in the tax-raising capacities of municipalities. Within a larger and more heterogeneous nation, a local income tax system will give rise to larger differential yields in different localities and will require, in the interest of fairness, other compensatory funding arrangements. An interesting facet of the Danish mechanism for equalising funding between municipalities is the principle that richer municipalities should transfer some of their 'excess fund raising' capacity to poorer communities. It prompts the question in English and Welsh contexts as to whether central government has discharged its funding responsibility in assessing the global amount to be made available to local government, and whether it is more legitimate to devolve to local authorities the responsibility for distributing these monies among themselves.

The Danish experience suggests that we would do well in this country to look critically at central government's underlying objective in funding local government services. The basic rationale of equalising inequalities in authorities' capacities to raise revenue must be regarded as paramount. The attempt to grapple with far more grandiose objectives from the centre has led to much complexity and undoubted arbitrariness. More seriously, it has threatened the very essence of local democracy.

Funding in England and Wales

During the past few years local government in England and Wales has been beset by a period of intense financial difficulty. Existing levels of expenditure have been curtailed and levels of local taxation increased. Coming hard on the heels of local government reorganisation, it has resulted in significant pressures on maintaining service priorities. It has been a period of difficult, and somewhat antagonistic, relationships between central and local government. All the indications are that the situation may deteriorate yet further. More difficulties, Royston Greenwood predicts, lie ahead: 'The Government's insistence on the new grant arrangements despite widespread resistance, and the inevitable confusion and resentment as the penalty clauses are invoked, will worsen rather than improve central-local relationships.'[4]

The shift of emphasis in central government preoccupations to an increasing involvement with the expenditure patterns of individual local authorities, rather than a more generalised concern for the total level of local government expenditure, has aroused considerable dismay in local government circles. A paper published by the Society of Local Authority Chief Executives concludes: 'The one point that can be made with certainty is that on the key issues . . . the Government has chosen control and influence by central government over individual local authorities, rather than reliance on local accountability within a national framework. This inevitably replaces local political control by new bureaucratic procedures.'[5]

Others fear a weakening of local accountability. A paper from the Institute of Local Government Studies says:

> Perhaps the central argument of Stewart and of Burgess and Travers is that the new financial systems will weaken and, more importantly, confuse local accountability by placing duties upon local authorities without giving them the powers to accomplish these responsibilities.[6]

Education which, in expenditure terms, is easily the largest local government service has been very much affected by, and in the forefront of, these difficulties. Indeed, the service implications in some areas of the country have been such that major doubts and considerable misgivings have been voiced as to whether, within the context of existing patterns of financing, it is possible to continue a sensible, meaningful and adequate level of educational provision.

The difficulties of recent years have been such as to make a comprehensive consideration of the future of local government finance appear essential. The warning signals of the past few years, the increasing disparities in the resources available to individual local authorities, are such as to make avoidance of its recurrence imperative. The ethos of this paper is rooted in the belief that there is a continuing meaningful role for local government, and that the education service is one of the major services which ought to continue within the ambit of local government. No doubt, some will question the possible optimism underpinning these statements. Nevertheless, they are the baseline from which the subsequent considerations of this paper stem.

Central government priorities in recent years have been focused upon the so-called 'battle against inflation'. Monetarist policies and the need to contain public expenditure patterns have been two of the keystones of such governmental perspectives. It has been asserted repeatedly by central government that without increased competitiveness on the international front the future economic prospects of the nation are very suspect and, in the short to medium term, the nation's resources ought to be rechannelled somewhat into the so-called 'wealth producing' section of the nation's activities. Further, it has been contended that the profligate spending patterns of some local and county councils cannot be allowed to usurp the vital national policies of the Government as they impinge on the containment of inflation, and that it has become unacceptable to allow such high expenditure patterns to continue unabated. This view has been re-echoed in certain contexts by industrial entrepreneurs and managers and, in particular, the concern of the Confederation of British Industry has been directed at the so-called increasingly unacceptable burden of local rates within the totality of industrial and commercial costs.

Given the range and force of some of the criticisms levelled at local government, it might be timely to ask some pertinent questions. From the educational vantage point, it is necessary to question whether the concept of a simple, yet sharp, division of the economy into a 'wealth producing' sector and an 'other' sector is valid in British societal realities of the 1980s. To view the whole process of education as unconnected with the quality of work and the strength of the economy is to do injustice to any real understanding of the nature of a technological society. Surely the most significant factor in any wealth production is the quality of human endeavour at all levels. To invest in the educational needs of young people – and in the continuing education of the community as a whole – is the most fundamental and relevant strategy for assuring any nation's future economic strength. The most apposite question would seem to be not whether the nation can afford to invest in education but rather whether it can afford not to invest in it. Certainly, there is scope for a full discussion on the precise nature of the educational priorities which are most relevant to our needs in present day society. However, this is not to be confused with an advocacy of a lower level of priority for education than hitherto.

Spending patterns

Another question which deserves consideration is whether public expenditure patterns have diminished in the past few years and, equally, whether overall expenditure on local government services has moved inexorably upwards.

Christopher Huhne in a recent article for *The Guardian* helps place the matter in its proper perspective:

> The increase in spending on social security – mostly on the unemployed but also on old people – accounts for the entire rise in the real total of public spending between 1978-9 and 1983-4, despite real cuts in individuals' entitlements. The other feature of the Government's public spending record is the pronounced shift from education (down $6\frac{1}{2}$ per cent) and housing (down 55 per cent) to defence (up 23 per cent) and law and order (up by 30 per cent).[7]

Reality indicates that the rise in public spending patterns has been attributable largely to the impact of unemployment and, as a consequence, it is central government rather than local government expenditure which has witnessed a real increase. Allied to this, there has been a clear and discernible reordering of central government spending priorities towards defence and law and order, and away from education and housing. If the Government is changing its priorities and diminishing the place of education in this reassessment, it is more sensible to start any discussion with this premise. Certainly, the facts are not consistent with a hypothesis of exaggerated and irresponsible expenditure upsurges by local government over recent years. Again, when considering the scenario for public expenditure over the next decade, it does not appear to be the continued provision of local government services which will provide the public expenditure pressures where the number of school age children is falling. Rather it is the view taken on future patterns of defence spending and an assumed growth rate too slow to reduce unemployment which are the key considerations. All this suggests that the crucial area for the achievement of a realistic level of public expenditure over the coming years is not the containing of local government expenditure but rather a creative and constructive approach to the problem of unemployment. Surely it is not beyond the efforts of our society to share available work for thirty million or so persons so as to provide a meaningful work outlet for another three million plus persons?

If the problem does not stem from local government expenditure patterns in general, what of the preoccupation of the Government with the expenditure patterns of individual councils? It is clear that the overall level of local government expenditure has not exhibited a significant upward trend in the past couple of years. Why in such circumstances is the Government so preoccupied with the spending patterns of a minority of so-called high spending councils (at least high spending in Government's evaluation if not in the view of their 'local electorates')? It is difficult to accept that a few high spending councils pose a major threat to the overall success of national economic policies. If so, the state of our economy must be more brittle than ever. Again, it is difficult to understand the logic of introducing an elaborately complex system of individual assessments of the amounts central government perceives individual councils ought to spend, coupled with an array of grant penalties – and possibly soon to be topped up with a limitation in some councils on how much rate precepts can be increased. If the intention is merely to curb the spending of a minority of councils this must be an extreme example of using a sledgehammer across the whole of local government to crack a nut.

Local democracy

The Government's approach here may appear to be one more manifestation of the most worrying feature affecting local government over the past decade, namely, the devaluation by successive central governments of the essence of local democracy. It seems imperative for those of all political persuasions who aspire to a role in national government to show an increased awareness and an enhanced sensitivity to the needs of local democracy. If it is felt valid within society for there to be freedom for individuals to decide on their priorities regarding spending patterns on a wide array of goods produced both at home and abroad, is it not equally valid for the same individuals collectively within their localities to express their preferences for higher standards of housing and health care for their families, better care for their elderly relatives, and improved education for their children? It does seem that the financial stranglehold being imposed upon individual local councils and the removal of the freedom of any significant voice in the determination of its overall level of expenditure (which will be the real impact of the proposed legislation of the present Government) poses a fundamental threat to the fabric of local democracy in this country.

If it is believed that local democracy should continue, and that a range of important decisions regarding the provision of certain services are best made at local rather than national level, it is necessary to look critically at the kind of financial approaches which will facilitate rather than inhibit the effective functioning of local democracy. In this respect, if it is felt that the rating system, as presently constituted, places unfair burdens on some sectors in the community such as the small businesses or the one person household, it is sensible to ask how the system of local financing can be modified. However, it is unhelpful to the future health of local democracy to confuse the defects and limitations of local finance as at presently constituted with an assertion, unfounded in the reality of recent years, that the present economic ills of the economy are due in large part to spiralling expenditure patterns in local government. Additionally, it has to be recognised that some of the ways in which successive central governments have fixed both the overall level and the distribution of finance for local councils have added significantly to the pressures on the local rating system. Some councils have had to raise their rate precepts markedly from one year to the next merely to maintain existing levels of service, after allowing for any impact of inflation, due to the annual vicissitudes of central government grant levels.

The difficulties – which can increase significantly in a complex society – inherent in any centralised apportionment of educational resources are highly significant and should not be underestimated. In pursuit of the resolution of such problems there is the ever-present danger that the financial mechanisms will become so complex as to be unintelligible to many involved in the associated decision-making. Equally dangerous is the fact that the overall assessment of needs is bedevilled by an inherent arbitrariness-cum-subjectivity. Further, a highly centralised financial approach (as epitomised by the present local government block grant with its individual GRE assessments and array of penalties) unaccompanied by a range of detailed legislative enactments to preserve minimum resourcing for a service, allows central government control without appropriate central government accountability. Again, the introduction of detailed regulations from the centre on such matters as class size is likely to affect significantly the central-cum-local balance of control over curricular matters.

Is there not a very real danger in the current discussions on the future of educational and local government finance that attention will be deflected from some fundamental considerations by an obsession with the block grant? Surely, as the Layfield Committee asserted some years ago, if local authorities are to have realistic and reasonable responsibility for localised services it is essential for them to have meaningful control over their financial destinies. Perhaps the argument needs to turn full circle and take as its starting point the requirements of a healthy local government system in practice. This is not to minimise the difficulties in current realities of achieving this objective, but it is to give precedence to long-term objectives over what may well be illusory short-term gains. John Stewart in an address to the Society of Education Officers touched upon these issues:

> The key to the complex government of education has been that power and authority have been diffused, with instruments geared to key issues linking actors and settings with the system. The movement from growth to constraints has made many of these instruments useless. The answer is not to seek new comprehensive instruments of control, but to rebuild self-governing systems guided by instruments of minimum control and maximum impact. It is the touch on the wheel that is required from the centre, not the detailed design. Instruments that are wider in impact than is required can harm in destroying the very diversity, initiative and responsiveness that justifies the local education authority as it does the local authority.[8]

In this quest for local democracy, it may be helpful to consider whether the only valid central government funding mechanisms are those of specific or block grants, and to dwell on alternative approaches to local taxation.

Central funding

The most difficult and awesome funding mechanism stems from an attempt by the centre to assess what expenditure patterns are desirable for each and every local authority. The larger and more heterogeneous the nation, the more complex the pattern of assessment must become. Clearly, given the diversity of influences both between and within services affecting spending needs, an elaborate array of factors, each with its own weighting for strength of effect, will need to be built into such assessment patterns. Certainly, the GRE assessments introduced by the current Government in England and Wales exhibit these characteristics and are epitomised by their statistical complexity which confound most local government members and officers – not to mention the population at large.

Possibly the most straightforward approach towards central government funding of local government is to be found in a relatively homogeneous nation where funding mechanisms focus upon equalising disparities in local funding. In other words, the main task is to ascertain whether there are significant variations between localities in their respective abilities to raise funds from available local taxes. Attention is concentrated not on the level of service provision required, but rather on the topping up of local taxation revenues so that all areas can obtain fairly similar yields per head of population from a particular level of taxation. It is the equalisation of inequalities in potential yields from local sources of finance which becomes the prime consideration of central government. It leaves the business of evaluating what levels of service provision are required to the local authorities themselves.

However, in some countries the national government has certain overriding responsibilities in terms of providing certain services, not least education. A range of legislative enactments places certain obligations upon central government to ensure a sensible and equitable service provision. A clear example is the need for national government in Britain to ensure that there is effective education for pupils of statutory school age. Until recent times, this has been interpreted as taking steps, financial and otherwise, to ensure a minimum level of service and an associated minimal level of funding. It is only in the last couple of years that national government in Britain has, through such measures as grant penalties, attempted to prescribe a maximum level of funding and, by implication, an upper level of service provision in such spheres as education. Consequently, the needs of a central government funding mechanism in England and Wales might be most sensibly given two main objectives, namely, the maintenance of minimum standards of provision and funding, and the eradication of significant disparities in local funding capacities. Clearly, the scope and nature of such central funding of local government is inexorably intertwined with the available sources of local taxation.

Grants: specific and block

Some would argue that the most sensible and appropriate mechanisms for central government funding are to be found in a range of specific grants. In this respect, a specific grant has been advocated for the funding of the totality of teachers' salaries. One significant requirement which is probably bound to accompany a range of specific grants for all local government services will be an influx of detailed legislative and administrative guidelines to local authorities. It is difficult to envisage central funding of teachers' salaries without the distinct possibility of national pronouncements on class size and on the range of curricular opportunities to be provided at differing ages. Such measures would represent, in large measure, centralised evaluations of local needs. It seems that of its essence a specific grant is designed to provide monies for defined purposes; it removes a local authority's freedom to evaluate how to spend the money it receives. Because of its specificity, there is a likelihood, even an obligation, upon national government to ensure the finance is delivered as intended. Hence, an array of specific grants is bound to operate within a detailed legislative/administrative framework.

Hitherto, the alternative consideration to the specific grant in England and Wales has been the block grant. This is a global sum of finance made available to local government to fund part of its services. Although the mode of allocation as between local authorities is determined by a complex statistical analysis, the finance can be used by individual authorities with considerable freedom as between its competing service priorities. Compared with a pattern of specific grants, there is much more residual freedom for local authorities in a block grant context to distribute available monies between the differing services. Possibly any reform of the current block grant funding needs to give much attention to two facets, namely, a major simplification in the calculation of available monies, and the 'opting out' by central government of the process of apportioning monies between the different local authorities.

The Norwegian experience in the funding of education gives some valuable insights into ways of achieving simplicity and intelligibility in the design of financial mechanisms. If the function of central government is to be seen largely as making sufficient available finance to ensure minimum standards of service provision within the nation, it can focus upon the global financial requirements and move away from a preoccupation with individual authority expenditure patterns. In such circumstances, it may be that one or two major factors can be highlighted for each service and used in the on-going global calculations. In the education context, as in Norway, teacher costs might be the critical dimension.

The whole issue of distributing available national government finance between local authorities might be better approached by devolving responsibility for this task to the national associations representing local authorities or to some independent board akin to the present arrangements in further/higher education. It would seem sensible to consider whether the present level of involvement of national government is too detailed in essence and whether there is scope for alternative approaches.

Assigned revenue

There is a possible alternative to the present grant system in England and Wales: one which would allow central government funding of local government to continue. It is the 'assigned revenue' approach to much of the funding of localised services. It has a very different, and possibly more sensible, philosophical underpinning. Instead of central government deciding the amount of finance to be made available to local government, the assigned revenue approach implies a joint dialogue between representatives of the two tiers of government with a view to reaching a coordinated and coherent agreed view as to which parts of available taxation should be allocated to fund central government services and which parts are needed to fund aspects of local government provision. There are two immediate advantages of an assigned revenue approach, namely, its relative ease and cheapness in implementation and the facility it offers for spreading expenditure allocations over a range of taxes so as to cohere with general national government taxation policies. Particularly if the assigned revenue approach is aimed at establishing the global amounts of money to be made available to local government, it is a system which has worked in other nations and has much to commend it. It warrants very serious detailed consideration in the current local government financial situation in England and Wales.

It is regrettable that the Government in its White Paper on the Rating System has seen fit to dismiss assigned revenues in just one paragraph as follows:

> Under assigned revenues, domestic rates would be replaced by an assigned share of the revenue from a national tax or taxes. This would be cheap to administer and would increase the ability of the Government to protect ratepayers from excessive local spending. But it would effectively eliminate any responsibility of local government for financing the services it provides. The Environment Committee therefore rejected this option, and the Government support their view.[9]

These comments merely confirm the somewhat blinkered preoccupation of the Government with alternatives to rates. What is needed instead is a critical analysis of all the requirements of local government finance.

Local taxation

The only source of local taxation available within local government is the property tax, known as the rates, which is levied on domestic and industrial properties. Certainly, pressures on the rates have grown in recent times largely because of a shift towards local funding away from national government grant. It seems vital here to reiterate that a considerable number of local authorities have had to raise rates significantly merely to continue existing patterns of services. As well as inflation, they have had to contend with a progressive cutback of central government funding.

One of the pressing needs in any coherent approach to local government finance is the need for a longer planning period. It is not conducive to effective local government to have sudden changes in the local government financial scenarios every few months. Cash limits, grant penalties, and alterations in the way monies are distributed between authorities have all contributed to this instability. Sensible and sensitive planning of essential services to the community (which is what local government is about) requires a longer than annual perspective. Local government, while needing to be very vigilant about efficiency, is not about profit making. It is about meeting vital community needs, and ought to be assessed and viewed in this light. To allow for cohesive planning, there ought to be high priority accorded to a three year approach to the funding of local government.

From a local vantage point, one of the basic limitations inherent in the rating system is that it accounts for too small a proportion of total local expenditure. A further drawback, in the context of a two-tier local government system, is that accountability between the tiers of local government becomes blurred in the eyes of the electorate since both tiers levy the same local tax. It is likely that, as far as the smaller local authorities are concerned, rates may well be the most sensible and propitious source of continuing local taxation. However, as far as the larger authorities are concerned (larger in terms of expenditure patterns) an alternative source of local taxation might be desirable. In Wales, for example, rates might continue to be the sensible pattern of local taxation for all other Councils, if an alternative source of local taxation could be found for the eight County Councils. The experience of other nations (particularly in Scandinavia), together with the conclusions from the detailed evaluation carried out by the Layfield Committee, point towards the introduction of a local income tax. As Layfield and his colleagues suggested:

> There is a strongly held view amongst us that the only way to sustain a vital local democracy is to enlarge the share of local taxation in total local revenue and thereby make councillors more directly accountable to local electorates for their expenditure and taxation decisions. On balance, we consider that the administrative cost involved in introducing a local income tax for this purpose would be justified. After many decades of uncertainty in the realm of local government finance the time has come for a choice on the issue of responsibility.[10]

It must be a source of some dismay to many in local government and outside that the present Government has abandoned the recommendation of its Environment Committee that it 'should take a decision to consider a local income tax' and thus commission further detailed study in the matter.

Whereas it is recognised that a local income tax could bring in its wake some difficulties for the Government in carrying out macro-economic management, a shift to an associated assigned revenue approach might allow meaningful dialogue to continue between the different tiers of government on the macro-economic needs of the nation. Again, it must be appreciated that the level of local government expenditure is such that much of income tax revenues would still be associated with central government. This brings with it problems of differentiating between 'local' and 'national' levies on income tax. The buoyancy of income tax is unlikely to mean large and sudden lurches in the amounts levied by local government. Again, the issue of differentiation in tax receipts – rates for smaller authorities and local income tax for larger authorities – warrants much further discussion.

Future prospects

Within the scope of this analysis it has been possible to pinpoint some critical considerations in the on-going dialogue about the future of local government finance. The main arguments may be summarised as follows:

1. To sustain a healthy local government it is axiomatic that considerable autonomy in local finance must be protected. To this end, the ability to raise a significant portion of necessary revenues from local taxation must be accorded a high priority.
2. Recognising the difficulties of implementation, it is nevertheless important to give due stress to the need to introduce new forms of local taxation. In this respect, a local income tax appears the most

sensible course of action. Further, it may be – particularly in the shorter term – that the poll taxes and the motor vehicle duty might be useful additions within local taxation.

3. It is vital to keep the recent strains placed on the rating system in perspective, and to appreciate its possible strengths as a continuing part of local taxation.

4. There is merit in giving further consideration to the concept of different forms of local taxation for different types of local authority. Might not local income tax be most relevant for the larger spending authorities, while rates continue as the local taxation base for smaller councils?

5. More emphasis ought to be given in the design of any financial instruments or systems to the twin objectives of simplicity and intelligibility. It is vital that those involved in decision-taking are not confronted with a statistical mystique which defies understanding.

6. It is not conducive to coherent financial and resource planning to base financial settlements and transfers on a one-year cycle. A much longer planning period is needed.

7. The time has come to look critically at the underlying objectives of central government funding of local government. Might the objectives focus on a global national evaluation of minimum levels of service provision and the need to iron out inequalities in the revenue raising capacities of different authorities? Ought not central government to leave the detailed distribution of funds between authorities to an independent body or to local authority associations?

8. It makes sense to evaluate the relative merits of the assigned revenue approach as a substitute for a block grant. The former might have important strengths in its philosophical base, its ease of implementation and – in the short to medium term – the advantage that it could cohere with a gradual move to a stronger local taxation base.

Many will contend that much of the above lacks political and financial realism. In answer, it is stressed that the real question is not whether we can afford a major reshape of local government finances but rather, whether for the future health of local democracy, we can afford not to overhaul the current system.

References

1. Kjell Eide (1976), *Financing Compulsory Education in Norway*, OECD.
2. Jack Springett (1982), *Why There is No Salvation in Block Grant*, Education (21 May 1982).
3. Erich Thoni, *The Basic Principles of the Austrian Financial Settlement*, University of Innsbruck.
4. Royston Greenwood, *Fiscal Pressure and Local Government in England and Wales* Chapter 4. Government Organisation and Structure in Hard Times.
5. Solace (1980), *The Local Government Bill*; Society of Local Authority Chief Executives.
6. Stewart Ranson (1980), *Changing Relations Between Centre and Locality in Education*. Inlogov.
7. Christopher Huhne (1983), Article in *The Guardian*.
8. J D Stewart (1982), Paper at Society of Education Officers Summer Meeting.
9. Department of the Environment/Welsh Office (1983), *White Paper: Rates*.
10. Report of the Committee of Enquiry (1972), *Local Government Finance*.

Acknowledgements

My thanks are due for help and cooperation to many people, and, in particular, to Elizabeth Rylance (British Council, Rome), Paul Lyngbye (Copenhagen), Herluf Rasmussen (Aarhus), Tomas Overgaard and Kjell Eide (Oslo), Werner Clement (Vienna), Peter Porsche (Klagenfurt), and Erich Thoni (Innsbruck).

Grateful appreciation is expressed to my Education Authority, West Glamorgan, for allowing my acceptance of this Fellowship, and to all colleagues within the Education Department for facilitating my work in this respect. Finally, a word of gratitude is due to my wife and family for support, patience and forbearance.

My own special interest in multi-cultural education has developed since moving to Derbyshire in 1981 as Area Education Officer. Working in a city which has a multi-ethnic population brought home to me the importance of educating all children for life in a culturally diverse society. In this country the issues involved are often addressed from an exclusively British standpoint, although immigration on a substantial scale has been common to all Western European countries since 1945.

It was the chance to gain a European perspective that decided me to apply for the AEC Trust Fellowship. I visited France, West Germany, the Netherlands, Belgium and Sweden, including the headquarters of the Council of Europe in Strasbourg and of the European Community in Brussels.

The tour was a great success from my point of view, broadening my own horizons, giving me contacts in different countries, and conferring, I hope, that European perspective on education for a multicultural society which I set out to achieve.

Peter Purnell

Chapter 5

Multicultural Education in Europe

Peter Purnell

Peter Purnell is Area Education Officer for Derby and South Derbyshire. He chose to examine arrangements for multicultural education in five other European countries. After teaching history in grammar and comprehensive schools, he entered educational administration with East Sussex County Council in 1971 working first as a professional assistant and, later, as deputy area education officer. His next move was to Dorset as assistant education officer in 1977. Peter Purnell took up his present post in 1981.

Immigration in Western Europe

The immigration experienced by all the European industrialised countries since 1945 has taken two forms: the permanent settlement in Britain, France and the Netherlands of citizens from their former colonies in South Asia, Africa and the Caribbean; and the temporary recruitment of migrant workers from southern Europe, Turkey and North Africa. About 15 million people of immigrant origin were living within the European Community countries in 1981. The table (page 108) shows the population from both sources in the countries I visited, and includes the UK for comparison (figures from UK 1981 Census and OECD 1980).

The two forms of immigration give rise to differences of outlook and terminology when multicultural education is considered from a European standpoint. In mainland Europe, policies are centred on the education of 'migrant' children, who are, in the main, foreigners in their country of residence. For that reason, the 1977 Directive of the European Community on the 'Education of the Children of Migrant Workers', which has been a powerful force for change within most EC

Immigration in six European countries

1980 (Thousands)	France	W. Germany	Netherlands	Belgium	Sweden	UK
Total Population	53,858	61,439	14,091	9,841	8,317	55,172

Total includes:

(1) Citizens from former colonial territories:

	France	W. Germany	Netherlands	Belgium	Sweden	UK
N. Africa, French origin	900					
N. Africa, Arab origin	350					
Other Africa	150					
Caribbean	400					
Far East	120					
Indonesia			300			
Moluccas			34			
Surinam/Caribbean			180			
Old Commonwealth						177
South Asia						655
Africa						267
Caribbean						295
Far East						136
Other New Commonwealth						160
	1,920 (Estimated)		514			1,690

(2) Foreign nationals

	France	W. Germany	Netherlands	Belgium	Sweden	UK
From EC countries:						
Italy	469	617	21	217	4	97
Greece	—	297	4	24	15	12
Eire	—	—	—	—	—	641
From other European countries:						
Portugal	857	112	10	10	2	16
Spain	424	180	24	64	34	40
Yugoslavia	68	631	14	—	39	13
Finland	—	10	—	—	181	—
From non-European countries:						
Turkey	103	1,462	106	59	18	12
Algeria	808	5	—	⎫ 77	—	2
Morocco	421	36	85	⎭	1	6
Tunisia	182	23	3	—	1	2
From all other countries:	814	1,077	214	523	127	1,071
	4,146	4,450	481	874		1,813

countries, is sometimes seen here as having little relevance to the educational issues raised by the presence of minority ethnic groups in the UK.

The Directive, which came into force on 25 July 1981, requires member states to provide for migrant children suitable reception facilities, language tuition and teacher training, and also to promote the teaching of the mother tongue and culture of origin in coordination with normal education. The EC has also sponsored a series of pilot schemes in various member states which have encouraged educational innovation and the exchange of ideas on ways of applying the Directive. These measures stem from growing concern about the social and educational situation of 'migrant' children, which led the EC countries to embark on a Social Action Programme in 1974 directed towards ensuring that migrants have equal opportunities with the citizens of member states.

The original expectation of the countries receiving migrant workers was that their labour requirements could be met by short-stay contracts without any significant implications for services like education. This view was confounded by the onset of economic recession in 1973 which brought a virtual halt to further migrant worker recruitment and an increasing stability of settlement among existing migrants. Their labour has become a structural feature of the advanced economies, while the migrants' own hopes of a return to their homelands has been diminished by adverse economic conditions there. As a result, the foreign populations of virtually all Western European countries have increased substantially during the past decade, largely owing to family reunions, high birth rates, and illegal immigration.

The education services of all the countries I visited have had to face up to a new challenge posed by a large and growing number of children and young people of different languages and cultures. The children of immigrants now account 'for a quarter of all births in the Western European industrialised countries – about 400,000 a year. Schools are increasingly educating children who are not themselves migrants but second generation immigrants, local-born like indigenous children but living within a different culture and usually speaking a different language when they are at home. The educational achievement of many of these children gives cause for concern. A disproportionate number have low levels of language proficiency and general attainment, often leading to placement in secondary schools with limited vocationally-based courses, or in special education; and frequently ending in failure to obtain school-leaving qualifications and unemployment.

The development of education policies

Although education policies in each country I visited have developed according to the country's own political response to the immigration situation, common threads can be discerned between them. While migrant workers were expected to return home within a limited period of time, education policies made few concessions to the situation of people of a different language and culture, other than the minimum necessary to ensure that they could function adequately during their stay. This usually meant little more than providing special instruction for children in school and for adult workers in the language of the host country.

At the same time, a system designed to maintain links with the language and culture of origin was set up throughout Europe, mainly on the basis of bilateral agreements between the receiving and sending countries. Under this system, foreign teachers are sent out for periods of up to six years to teach the children of their own nationality, either as part of the school curriculum or outside normal school hours. France, Belgium, some of the West German states, and even Britain to a limited extent (in the form of teachers provided by the Italian consulates for after-school classes) operate this system. However, the Netherlands, Sweden, and other West German states prefer to recruit the foreign teachers required to teach classes in the language and culture of origin from among their own immigrant communities, both to avoid the political influence exercised by undemocratic regimes and to exercise greater control over the conduct of classes.

Quite apart from these special measures for migrant children, education policies in Western Europe have been influenced in varying degrees by the concept of 'intercultural education' which has developed since the mid-1970s, stimulated by the work of educationalists in different countries and by the international seminars and reports organised by the Council of Europe through its Council for Cultural Cooperation. 'Intercultural education' means the building of an understanding and acceptance of different cultures into the educational process of *all* pupils. It requires knowledgeable and sensitive teachers and also curricula, methods and materials which are appropriate to the education of children growing up in culturally diverse societies. Intercultural education is therefore similar in concept to 'education for a multicultural society', a term often used in Britain. 'Multicultural education' is used specifically in mainland Europe to describe the education provided in a society which contains a number of ethnic groups and implies no particular policy direction.

France

Despite government attempts after 1974 to restrict immigration, and under former President Giscard d'Estaing to encourage repatriation, the number of foreign pupils in the French state school system rose from 694,000 in 1974/75 to 912,000 in 1980/81, about nine per cent of the total school population. Official statistics refer only to 'foreign' or 'immigrant' pupils, thereby excluding the substantial number of French children of African and Caribbean origin. The areas centred on Paris, Lyon/Grenoble, and Marseille/Côte d'Azur have the highest concentrations of immigrants, particularly those from the Arabic-speaking countries of Algeria, Morocco and Tunisia who together make up half of France's foreign school population, and whose educational attainment gives cause for the greatest concern.

French policy on the education of foreign children has concentrated on the rapid learning of French. A small proportion of foreign pupils are taught in special initiation classes or in withdrawal groups, but the great majority learn French in normal classes from teachers who have in theory benefited from the new courses and methods devised by the Office for the Instruction of Foreigners in French Language and Civilisation (BELC) and the Study and Research Centre for the Dissemination of the French Langauge (CREDIF). The emphasis within the education system on the assimilation of French language and culture is pronounced, though since 1975 there has been Ministry of Education encouragement for the inclusion within the school time-table of the three hours a week supplementary classes in the principal minority languages which are more usually held in 'parallel' classes outside normal school hours. In either case, the foreign teachers are employed directly by the sending countries, and usually have very little influence on the standard French curriculum.

From 1978, however, the circulars of the Ministry of Education reveal a significant shift in official attitude. They give a clear lead to schools and to the regional authorities and local inspectors by emphasising the importance of other languages and cultures to the work of all schools and urging fuller use of the agreements with foreign governments for setting up mother-tongue classes within the time-table. The Ministry also stresses the need for suitable reception arrangements for foreign children and for good home/school liaison, and also draws attention to the role of the regional centres for the information and training of staff concerned with teaching migrant children (CEFISEM) in developing intercultural education.

The first CEFISEM was established at Lyon in 1975, and there are now 14 of them situated in the major centres of foreign population. I visited the centres in Grenoble and Marseille. The CEFISEM teams, which comprise a special section of the primary teacher training college for their area, work through courses and school visits to 'sensitise' teachers to cultural differences among their pupils and to their own ethnocentric attitudes, and to advise them on bringing an intercultural perspective to their teaching. This work is aided by the Documentation Office on Migrants, established in Paris in 1973, which distributes a monthly bulletin containing information about minorities, and a quarterly review publicising educational developments in the field of immigrant education.

In 1981 the Mitterand Government introduced education priority zones under which schools in socially deprived areas, which include districts with over 30 per cent foreign children, can receive extra staffing to reduce class sizes and improve home–school links. The aim is to reduce the educational under-achievement which is felt to contribute towards the high unemployment rate among young people, particularly foreigners. I joined a discussion between teachers of a primary school near Marseille on ways of developing the school's community involvement, which included establishing a municipal library at the school with the focus on 'intercultural' books. In Marseille itself I visited schools in the Frais-Vallon district where, as an EC pilot project in 1979–82, mother-tongue teaching in Italian and Arabic had been integrated into the nursery school (90 per cent of French children aged 2–6 attend the impressive system of *écoles maternelles*) and primary school (ages 6–11). Parents were encouraged to help with activities featuring artefacts and music from minority cultures. The schools here were also more involved with the community than appears usual in France.

The secondary sector (comprehensive schools 11–16, *lycées* 16–19, with vocational alternatives from 14-plus) appears to be largely untouched by the concept of intercultural education. Portuguese, Spanish, Italian and Arabic are available as foreign languages, but, as these have to be taught by French teachers, opportunities are limited in practice for foreign pupils who wish to study their mother-tongue within the secondary school curriculum.

I formed the impression that, despite official encouragement, intercultural education has so far made little impact on traditional practice within the French education system. Developments appear to be based on the formative work on intercultural education and teacher training by staff at CREDIF and the higher teachers' college at St. Cloud (particularly that of Louis Porcher for the Council of Europe), the influence of some enlightened administrators, and the commitment of teachers working in the regional CEFISEMs, rather than on school-led initiatives.

Interestingly, the particular situation of black French children is rarely considered in discussion on the education of immigrant pupils, though they often experience similar educational difficulties. Racism does not appear to be recognised as an educational issue, though it is now becoming the subject of public discussion owing to social tensions fuelled by economic recession and also to the growing evidence of lack of real equality of opportunity for second generation immigrants.

West Germany

Education policies in the German Federal Republic make considerable provision for 'the children of foreign workers'. There is no official acceptance of intercultural education, although 12 per cent of the children attending primary schools (ages 6–10) in the Federal Republic are foreign, a figure rising to 33 per cent in West Berlin and 85 per cent in some urban areas. There were in all 638,000 foreign pupils in the compulsory school system in 1980–81.

The Federal Government's policy is to restrict the immigration of foreigners and encourage repatriation, while at the same time improving the economic and social integration of those who have lived in the Federal Republic for a number of years. Accordingly, regulations governing the education of foreign workers' children, agreed in substance as long ago as 1971 by the eleven federal states which have virtual autonomy in education matters, emphasise both the maintenance of links with the language and culture of origin and – increasingly in recent years – measures to promote the integration of foreign children into the mainstream school system.

The regulations state that foreign children should normally be placed in a regular German class according to their level of education, receiving, where necessary, extra tuition in German for up to ten hours a week either in place of other subjects in the curriculum or in extra-curricular classes held in the afternoons. Preparatory classes can be formed if there are at least ten pupils with insufficient knowledge of German for immediate placement in regular classes. However, foreign children quite often complete their secondary education in 'preparatory classes'. Special classes for foreign pupils are encouraged if the proportion of foreign pupils in regular classes would otherwise exceed 20 per cent. This figure has now been relaxed to 50 per cent in West Berlin, for example, because of the high concentration of foreigners in certain districts.

Classes for foreign pupils in their own language and culture, whether taught by foreign teachers employed through the consulate system as in six of the federal states, or directly by the state government as in the other five, do not appear to influence the normal German curriculum. The lessons are generally held after the end of morning school or in the afternoons, but can be included in the curriculum of the preparatory or special classes for foreign pupils if these consist of children with a common first language. In Bavaria, the policy is to direct foreign pupils into monolingual classes in which the mother tongue is the main medium of instruction. I heard a good deal of criticism of this system elsewhere in Germany on the grounds that it gives priority to the re-integration of foreign pupils into the country of origin at the expense of leaving them ill-prepared for life in the Federal Republic.

I visited schools and talked to teachers, researchers and administrators in Baden-Würtemburg, North Rhine-Westphalia, Lower Saxony, Hesse, West Berlin and Hamburg. It was plain that substantial educational provision is being made for foreign children. The measures taken include the following: 1 Extra teaching staff to reduce class sizes and provide remedial and supplementary courses – Baden-Würtemburg, with 115,000 foreign pupils, had 2,250 extra full-time posts in 1981–82; 2 A large-scale in-service training programme – North Rhine-Westphalia, with 275,000 foreign pupils, currently provides special training for 5,000 teachers a year, backed by curriculum material produced by its Centre for Educational Resources and Development; 3 'Socialisation' measures, including a drive to encourage foreign parents to enrol their children in a kindergarten (ages 4–6), one-term pre-school courses to prepare foreign children for primary school – I visited one such school in the Kreuzberg area of West Berlin which had care facilities from 6.00 a.m.–6.00 p.m. – and

homework sessions supervised by foreign teachers or ancillaries;
4 Distribution of education information in appropriate languages to
foreign parents and encouragement to schools to develop their home
links.

The aim of this provision is to improve the poor educational
performance of some national groups, and particularly children of
Turkish origin. The size of the Turkish population (over 1.5 million),
its rate of growth (by 1985 every tenth child in West German schools
will be Muslim), its high level of educational under-achievement, and
comparative lack of social integration creating tensions among the host
community all present a major challenge to the Federal Republic. Difficulties are most pronounced among young adults, for employment
prospects in West Germany are bleak for those without the basic
school-leaving certificate, possession of which has until very recently
carried the virtual guarantee of a recognised occupation, linked with
compulsory part-time further education. Failure rates of up to 50 per
cent have provided a major spur to action throughout the education
system, and provision of second-chance opportunities in the
impressive system of vocational schools, which correspond roughly to
our further education sector. Of the 218 experimental projects in the
field of foreign children's education funded during the past 13 years by
the Federal Government at a cost of approximately £50 million, many
of the most recent have been directed towards preparing young
foreigners for employment.

The most interesting intercultural education developments I saw
were in North Rhine–Westphalia and West Berlin. (Hesse and West
Berlin are the only two States with a significant number of comprehensive schools as an alternative to the tripartite secondary selective
system.) North Rhine–Westphalia is developing an Islamic religious
education syllabus; the principal minority languages can now be
included in the secondary curriculum as alternative foreign languages,
though only up to age 16; and in some Essen primary schools, German
teachers who had learned some Turkish were using bilingual
approaches with young children. An interesting development was the
RAA, a system of centres for the education of foreign children and
young people established in eight Ruhr cities, which combine the
preparation of intercultural resources material with teacher training in
cultural diversity and home-school liaison. There are some similarities
with the work of the CEFISEM in France, though the strongest
influence on the development of the RAA has come from its links with
Coventry.

West Berlin, which has the highest concentration of Turks in the Federal Republic, is developing secondary course books with a dual German–Turkish text, a project receiving national and EC financial support. Some in-service courses for German and foreign teachers are being combined with the aim of fostering intercultural co-operation, and enterprising home–school liaison initiatives are being encouraged. I visited an all-day comprehensive school in West Berlin which had structured its staff into year teams, each with a Turkish teacher, which provided all the teaching for that particular year group and set out to create strong links with parents in the belief that only by adapting the traditional school situation to a more family-type unit could the Turkish children realise their potential. This school was, however, atypical as few real concessions were, I felt, made to the cultural situation of foreign pupils. Education measures generally in the Federal Republic are largely directed towards pupils' assimilation into the German education system.

The Netherlands

The Dutch have traditionally maintained a liberal attitude towards immigrants, and this is reflected in their educational policies for 'ethnic minorities'. This term embraces migrant workers (with Turks and Moroccans predominating), black citizens from the Dutch Antilles and Surinam, Moluccans, gypsies and foreign refugees – but not the 300,000 Indonesians who are regarded as integrated into Dutch society. There were 88,500 minority pupils at Dutch nursery and primary schools in 1980, 5.1 per cent of the total.

Schools with ethnic minority pupils receive, as well as extra capitation allowance, supplementary staffing on a graduated scale which gives nursery (ages 4–6) and primary (6–12) schools an extra teacher if they have between 16 and 24 immigrant children who have lived in the Netherlands for less than two years. A different scale gives primary schools extra staffing on a longer-term support basis for minority children who have lived longer in the Netherlands – roughly on the basis of half a day for every ten children. There is also a scale, linked to parental occupation, giving supplementary staffing to schools in socially disadvantaged areas. The effect of all these supplementary scales is to give all the schools I saw class sizes very much smaller than the 1:32 standard teacher–pupil ratio.

In the secondary school system minority children tend to gravitate towards the lower vocational schools, at some of which 'international bridging classes' are provided for non-Dutch-speaking children. From there, the chances of upward educational mobility seemed slight, though the school I visited in Amsterdam also provides older students with second-chance opportunities through day and evening classes. Some supplementary staff time is also devoted to furthering contacts with the parents of foreign and West Indian/Surinamese pupils. This apart, the secondary sector generally seems little influenced by developments towards intercultural education – but that was typical of all the countries I visited.

The Dutch Government's Policy Programme for Ethnic Minorities (1981) marks a significant change from the previous policy document 'Education and Training of Migrants' (1976) which had rejected the idea that the Netherlands could be other than a temporary home for migrant workers and had adopted an 'assimilation' policy towards the education of their children. The 1981 Policy Programme accepts that 'most members of ethnic minorities will remain in the Netherlands for a long time, if not for good', and addresses itself to measures which are appropriate to the education of children in a plural society. Schools receiving extra resources for minority children are expected to produce an action plan setting out their aims and methods, to improve their home–school liaison, and to encourage parents to enrol for adult education. In a multicultural quarter in Amsterdam, I visited a project team of seconded teachers working on the development of teaching materials and supporting class teachers on intercultural approaches and home visiting.

Schools are also required to integrate into the normal curriculum the two lessons a week of home language and culture provided by foreign teachers employed by the Dutch authorities. There are about 1,300 foreign teachers in the Netherlands, and a feature of some schools I visited was the important contribution being made to inter-cultural education in the classroom by the professional contacts between the Dutch and the foreign teachers, who at present receive equal pay and will soon have equality of status as well when they are recognised as teachers rather than 'education assistants'. The Ministry of Education has been active in establishing courses for foreign teachers and for Dutch teachers teaching foreign children, while a number of initial teacher training courses now include intercultural education as an integral element.

The most interesting mother-tongue teaching I observed was in Enschede, in an experimental scheme partly EC-financed. Turkish and Moroccan children receive some bilingual teaching in certain nursery schools and are then grouped for their first two years of primary education in order to follow a bicultural curriculum. This comprises some teaching in mother tongue by a Turkish or Moroccan teacher, some Dutch teaching by a Dutch teacher, and 'integration lessons' with the parallel group of Dutch children. The staff were convinced that under this system the foreign children progress into regular classes more confident and better prepared to follow the normal syllabus, while continuing to receive teaching in home language and culture for one or two periods a week.

In September 1982 the Ministry of Education published an Educational Priority Plan, in conjunction with the Ministry of Welfare, Health and Cultural Affairs. Under the plan, existing arrangements for extra resources to support ethnic minorities will be brought within a wider framework of measures, including the designation of educational priority areas, designed to combat the educational disadvantage resulting from economic and social deprivation. Underprivilege is seen as a major additional handicap to many ethnic minority children on top of specific cultural factors such as language problems and the conflict of values between home and school.

The consensus which exists in the Netherlands, except among extremist groups, in favour of positive action for ethnic minorities has undoubtedly assisted the Government in devoting resources (about £45 million in 1980) to their particular needs and in developing new policies. The Ministry of Education has considerable powers of central direction over the schools' organisation and curriculum, arising perhaps from the fragmented nature of local management in education, under which municipal and district councils control only about a quarter of the schools in their areas, the remainder being run by separate school boards for Catholic (37 per cent), Protestant (26 per cent) and non-denomination (11 per cent) schools. All four sectors receive an appropriate share of funding from the Ministry, which regulates the school system through its locally-based state inspectors. Only the larger towns have their own advisory teams, and it was in some of these I saw evidence that intercultural education was being prompted by local initiative and committed teachers. Dordrecht, for example, established a Bureau for Ethnic Minorities eight years ago, the first in Holland, where eight staff provide local in-service training, work on intercultural teaching materials, produce an information bulletin, and help with translation services.

In *The Dutch Plural Society* (1973), Christopher Bagley contrasted the traditional racial tolerance and harmony of Dutch society with the evidence of racial discrimination in Britain. Ten years on, I found that racial harmony in the Netherlands is subject to increasing tensions. As the second generations of black Dutch people, Turks and Moroccans grow up in the Netherlands, race may come to the fore as an educational issue unless the Government's Educational Policy Plan is successful in making an impact on ethnic disadvantage in education by changing, for example, a situation in which 40 per cent of ethnic minority pupils fail to obtain a school-leaving certificate.

Belgium

After Luxembourg (26 per cent) and Switzerland (15 per cent), Belgium has proportionately the third highest foreign population in Western Europe at 10 per cent, of which just under half are 'migrants'. In Brussels itself the proportion of foreigners is 27 per cent. In the 0–9 age group, foreign children account for 16 per cent of the country's population, rising to 40 per cent in Brussels.

The Belgian Government's official stance is that Belgians and foreigners have equal rights and opportunities under the education system. In practice, as in all the countries I visited, the normal institutional processes of selection by school attainment, language proficiency and cultural level combine to disadvantage some migrant children, particularly those who have moved during their years of schooling. Nonetheless, the Italian community, which comprises about half the migrant worker population in Belgium, is comparatively well integrated, owing to traditional links with the Belgian coal fields stretching back to the 1920s. Many Italians living in Belgium are second or third generation residents, and their participation rate in post-compulsory and higher education exceeds that of Belgian pupils. Their situation, and that of Spanish and Greek children, contrasts with that of Moroccan and Turkish pupils, who generally fare badly in the Belgian education system.

Until 1976 there were no systematic reception arrangements for foreign children in Belgian schools. Since then, pressure to relieve growing unemployment among Belgian teachers, combined with the need to meet the requirements of the 1977 EC Directive on the Education of Migrant Workers' Children, has led to the introduction of a system of supplementary staffing for schools. In nursery and primary schools with over 30 per cent migrant children, those of nursery age $(2\frac{1}{2}-6)$ who are not fluent in the language of instruction count double for staffing purposes, while primary children (ages 6–12) count 1.5 for the first two years and 1.3 thereafter. This system enables separate adaptation classes to be set up for foreign children. Primary teachers who are supernumerary to established posts owing to the fall in the birth rate are also used for supportive language work with small groups. However, I observed a number of migrant children of secondary age in primary classes, which raises questions about the appropriateness for foreign pupils of a system which relates annual progression to attainment levels. More than half of the foreign pupils in Belgian primary schools have to repeat at least one year, as against a third of Belgian children.

In the selective secondary system extra staffing can be provided for four hours' additional language work a week with foreign pupils who have had less than the full primary school course and whose language proficiency is inadequate, on the basis of one teacher for ten pupils, two for 16–30 pupils, and thereafter one for every 15 pupils. It is questionable how far this system is meeting the needs of foreign children, a substantial number of whom leave school at 14 with no qualifications and few job prospects. A number of voluntary schools, run by private associations, have sprung up to try to give their mainly Turkish and Moroccan pupils some of the language and pre-vocational skills needed to improve their life chances. I visited such a school in Brussels which provided for 14–17 year olds unable to benefit from mainstream education a range of practical courses linked with core subjects, social education, and tuition in French and the mother tongue. A special feature was the provision of apprenticeship places for renovation work on public and private buildings under a scheme financed by the EC and the Ministry of Education.

The difficulties of foreign children in Belgium are compounded by the language laws, which make Dutch the local language in Flanders, French the official language in Wallonia, and Brussels itself a bilingual region. There are special provisions for the German-speaking region and for areas with large French or Dutch-speaking minorities. The language which is not the official language is introduced as the compulsory second language at age nine in bilingual regions (and on an optional basis elsewhere), and must be followed throughout the school career except in certain technical and vocational schools. This means many foreign children must master not only one but two foreign languages to earn places in the general secondary schools and entry to higher education and many employment opportunities.

Since 1977, foreign children in Belgium have been able to have lessons in their language and culture of origin, mainly outside the normal curriculum, from foreign teachers supplied through the embassies of the various countries concerned. The familiar difficulties of organising mother-tongue teaching outside the normal timetable have led to patchy provision, leaving a great deal to the initiative of individual schools or authorities in making arrangements.

An exception is the Limburg area where lessons in Turkish, Greek and Italian have been integrated into the curriculum of several primary schools, initially as an EC-financed pilot scheme. This project represents more than just the inclusion of minority languages within the timetable, but a bicultural approach to the education of foreign children. The lesson content of the four hours' teaching in the language and culture of origin, which reduces to two hours in the upper primary years, is coordinated between all the different language groups, including the Dutch. This scheme has now been extended to 20 schools with support from the Limburg province, and discussions are under way about introducing it to six secondary schools.

A key element in the success of bicultural schemes is the degree of effective communication between the indigenous and foreign teachers. In this case a major constraint is the contract basis on which foreign teachers are supplied in Belgium, which means that they have often just attained a command of Dutch, learned to adjust to the pedagogical expectations of the school, and got to know the other teachers by the time their contracts end.

In Brussels some of the local authorities (the local management of education is, as in the Dutch system, in the hands of over 500 municipalities, together with school boards for denominational and free schools) have begun to recruit their own foreign teachers from among the immigrant population and to use them in combination with Belgian teachers for integrated work in primary schools in the official language and the mother tongue. I also visited a secondary school which was experimenting with classes of foreign children following the same curriculum as the Belgian children and being taught by Belgian teachers, but with the assistance of bilingual auxiliaries.

Belgian teachers have considerable freedom within the outline syllabuses authorised by the Ministries of Education (the cultural divide is such that there are separate ministries for the French and Dutch-speaking areas). I was impressed by some imaginative organisation and teaching which was clearly influenced by the aims of intercultural education. This stemmed from local initiatives by committed teachers and inspectors, rather than from official policies, which appear to give no encouragement to intercultural education. A constraint on the spread of ideas is the lack of any systematic in-service training for teachers. Although there has been an EC-financed course on the education of foreign children at Louvain University for 270 teachers, it is not clear how Belgium will meet its obligation under the EC Directive to prepare teachers generally for working with the children of migrants.

Sweden

Sweden seems to have largely eliminated, through progressive social policies financed by economic growth and high taxation, the economic and social deprivation which afflicts a significant proportion of the immigrant populations in other states. The emphasis on social equality, so evident in Swedish life, produced from 1975 onwards legislation designed to give effect to three principles enunciated by a national Commission on Immigration: equality of opportunity for minorities; freedom of choice to maintain and develop their culture and language of origin; and partnership between the different groups which make up Swedish society.

The majority of immigrants to Sweden are from other Nordic countries, mainly Finland, although extra-European immigration rose during the 1970s from eight per cent to 31 per cent of the total, owing to Sweden's liberal policy towards the admission of refugees. Although foreign nationals account for under five per cent of the Swedish population of 8.3 million, naturalised immigrants and other citizens of foreign extraction double, to nearly one million, the number of Swedish residents of non-indigenous origin.

The drive for equality for minorities covers the whole range of social policy, but in education it is concentrated on measures to enable them to achieve full participation in Swedish life, largely in the form of support for learning Swedish and for the nurturing of minority languages with the stated goal of 'active bilingualism'.

The 1977 Home Language Reform placed an obligation on local authorities (279 municipalities backed by 24 counties, under the policy-making National Board of Education) to provide mother-tongue teaching, if desired, as part of the school curriculum for all children if at least one parent speaks a language other than Swedish at home. This requirement extends from pre-school education (for six-year-olds), through the compulsory comprehensive school (age range

7-16, organised in three levels, junior, intermediate and senior), into the integrated upper secondary school (a tertiary college-type institution attended by almost 90 per cent of Swedes). By 1982/83, 55,000 out of 86,000 eligible pupils of compulsory school age were receiving home language teaching in one of 63 different languages. The programme is staffed by teachers recruited mainly from among minority groups living in Sweden, given a two-year training course at universities designated for specific languages, and appointed mainly on a peripatetic basis to work in several schools at a salary scale higher than that of primary teachers.

Home language teaching is provided in three forms, depending on numbers: the **withdrawal** of pupils from normal classes, as individuals or in groups of up to four, for two lessons a week mother-tongue teaching, to which may be added study guidance through the medium of mother tongue in various subjects, and also supportive Swedish lessons from a Swedish teacher; the **composite class** consisting of about half Swedish pupils and half pupils having a common minority language, who are taught separately in the mother tongue for about 60 per cent of the timetable in the first year of compulsory school, after which the proportion of the time taught in the minority language declines to four/five lessons a week between ages 10-13; and the **home language class** consisting entirely of pupils sharing a common mother tongue in which teaching is begun in that language with Swedish being introduced as a second language at age nine. For all children Swedish becomes the sole teaching medium at senior level (13-16), though minority pupils may continue with two lessons a week home language teaching as under the first model. However, a number of minority languages can also be studied as part of the foreign languages curriculum up to examination level.

In visits to schools in the Stockholm district, Gothenburg and Nörrköping, I observed various forms of home language teaching in Finnish, Assyrian, Serbo-Croatian, Spanish and English (which is also the first compulsory foreign language, introduced at age nine) and was impressed by the strength of commitment to bilingualism among teachers, organisers, researchers and administrators. The Swedes are evaluating the bilingual programme carefully and the results so far indicate that minority children educated in home language and composite classes are not inferior in their knowledge of Swedish at age 16 when compared with their peers taught solely in Swedish, though they more often need support at 13 or 14; that their personal and intellectual development is likely to be superior; and that they are genuinely bilingual, which is officially regarded as a personal, cultural and social asset.

Support for the learning of home language and Swedish as a second language also permeates the highly-developed and mainly free or subsidised system of basic literacy programmes, municipal adult education, workplace and community-based study circles, and the 110 folk high schools. Swedish employers are legally required to grant 240 hours' paid study leave a year to employees whose Swedish is inadequate. Immigrants also benefit from the impressive system of labour market training, which provides youth training schemes for the minority of 16 to 18-year-olds who are not receiving full-time education in the integrated upper secondary school, and 53 skills centres for adults, the fourth largest of which I visited in Nörrköping.

The Swedish Government has set up a number of commissions to evaluate its reforms and to recommend further steps towards creating a just society for minority groups. These include the Commission on Immigration Research, the Commission on Ethnic Prejudice and Discrimination, the Commission on Linguistic Minorities of Pre-School Age, the Commission on Migrants' Languages and Culture in School and Adult Education, as well as a Commission on Immigration Policy. I came away with the impression that Swedish policy is moving towards embedding bilingualism into the fabric of school and society, despite some fears about ethnic autonomy; progressing beyond its concentration on language into the so far neglected field of intercultural education, by stipulating as a first step its inclusion in the training of all school staff; and attempting to secure improvements in the employment situation of immigrants, whose unemployment rate at about eight per cent is double the national average.

European trends in multicultural education

The chief impression arising from my visits to other European countries is that there is a convergent trend between those countries which are coming to terms with the long-term presence of 'migrant' populations and those, like the UK, which have permanently settled citizens of overseas origin. The differences in terminology and citizenship status between children of migrant workers and of ethnic minorities have obscured the underlying similarities between their educational and social situation.

There is really no difference in the practical task facing education authorities and teachers in the multicultural societies which now exist in Britain and the other countries of Western Europe. That is how to give children from different linguistic and cultural backgrounds an equal chance to succeed in school and society. That task, which initially seemed less important to countries which received migrant workers because of the anticipated limited period of stay, has assumed progressively greater significance during the past decade with the growing realisation that many of the children of migrant workers, who are now increasingly second generation immigrants, are there to stay, if not permanently, at least for a long time. Furthermore, the emphasis on the maintenance of foreign children's own language and culture, whose main purpose was to aid re-integration into the country of origin, has begun to shift to take account of the educational case for including mother-tongue and bilingual teaching within the normal curriculum, at a time when there is a growing interest in the UK in utilising the resource of minority languages in schools.

This European trend is reflected in the recommendations of the Standing Conference of European Ministers of Education, which normally meets every two years, and for which the Council of Europe provides the secretariat. The Strasbourg conference in 1974 concentrated on ways of solving the educational and training 'problems' of migrant children without showing much appreciation of the cultural factors which affect their achievement. However, the Dublin conference in May 1983 agreed to recommend member states to take positive action to meet the educational and cultural needs of migrants with the aim of providing equality of opportunity; to encourage the maintenance of migrants' cultural links, not just to facilitate their return to their country of origin, but to foster their own development and their contribution to the society in which they are resident; to aim to achieve an intercultural dimension in education through curriculum development; to arrange for all host country teachers to increase their awareness of the benefits of and obstacles to intercultural understanding; and to intensify their research into intercultural education, including bilingualism, rigidity of cultural attitudes, and racism.

Multicultural education in Britain

The language and outlook of the Dublin conference recommendations are readily recognisable within the context of developments in multicultural education in Britain where attitudes have changed significantly during the past two decades in response to the presence of ethnic minorities. There has been a shift from the assimilationist view that immigrant children could be fairly easily absorbed into the education system with some initial help where necessary with the learning of English. During the 1970s schools had been encouraged to adapt their organisation, curriculum and materials in order to take account of the fact of cultural diversity in Britain. *Education in Schools: a Consultative Document* (DES, 1977) stated: 'Our society is a multi-cultural, multiracial one and the curriculum should reflect a sympathetic understanding of the different cultures and races that now make up our society', a view reinforced in the *School Curriculum* (DES, 1981). Some LEAs have gone beyond an acceptance of cultural diversity and adopted a perspective based on equality, which requires changes of attitude of a more fundamental nature among the majority culture in order to free ethnic minority children from the 'institutional racism' by which schools and other educational institutions are held to discriminate, albeit unwittingly, against ethnic minorities in the way they operate.

Yet the Schools Council report *Multi-Ethnic Education: The Way Forward* (1981) revealed a considerable gap between stated policies on multicultural education and practice within schools. The report showed that efforts were concentrated on the basic requirement of teaching English to non-English-speaking children, and that there was limited support for other needs of ethnic minority children. Moreover, many schools in areas containing few or no ethnic minority children were said to have done little to prepare their pupils for life in a multi-cultural society, while even in areas with medium to high concen-trations of ethnic minority pupils, much of the work in schools was said to have been based on traditional approaches which pay little regard to the cultural background of their pupils.

The gap between stated policies and what is actually going on in schools shows that teacher attitudes are crucial to real progress in multicultural education. The gap can be narrowed where change has originated amongst teachers or where they have a clear understanding of the processes. The commitment in some countries to the inclusion of intercultural education in the initial training course of all teachers and to systematic in-service training programmes for the teachers of foreign children makes the situation in Britain look patchy and un-coordinated by comparison. Here, the separation and relative decentralisation of responsibility for initial and in-service training requires a clear lead from the DES if the proper priority is to be accorded to multicultural education in the training of teachers.

In the countries I visited the stance adopted by governments in their public statements, their policies, and their allocation of resources has been influential in shaping developments within schools in the field of multicultural education. A clear-cut commitment by government to the aims of intercultural education is particularly important in generating a climate of opinion which encourages positive attitudes not only among teachers but also teacher trainers, education advisers and administrators.

Second language learning

In meeting the particular needs of both foreign and ethnic minority pupils, the highest priority in all the countries I visited, as in Britain, is given to the acquisition of the language of the 'host' country. However, the way in which this is provided shows certain differences of approach. Alongside immersion in the normal school system, a process mostly supported by a variety of special measures, there are some features which imply segregation in that migrant workers' children are isolated from mainstream education in various forms of special class. In some cases, the cultural protection of indigenous children appears to be the main motive for this. But where the aim of the special class is to prepare foreign children for successful integration into normal schooling by means of an intensive introductory language course the separation often appears to be counter-productive because of the difficulty of transition to mainstream education later on.

Research commissioned by the EC to evaluate its pilot schemes on the application of the 1977 Directive on the Education of the Children of Migrant Workers favoured early integration of foreign children into normal classes provided they are given intensive assistance inside and outside the classroom (*ALFA Research Group – Essen/Landau, 1980. XII/954/80 – EN*). This has implications for the reception and language centres which provide for seven per cent of the 104,000 school-age children in Britain who come from homes where English is not the first language.

Of course, the great majority of such children now start school in this country and learn English through attending normal classes with specialist support, staffed by the equivalent of 1,900 full-time additional teachers 75 per cent funded by government under the 1966

Local Government Act, together with ordinary class teachers. Provision for second language teaching in this country generally compares well with that of most of the countries I visited, but there are certain features which Continental and particularly Swedish experience suggests could be improved on. The first is better support for pupils' language development beyond the stage of initial proficiency, and across the range of curriculum subjects, to encourage the attainment of the standards of literacy required at examination level and for entry to further and higher education and wider opportunities in adulthood. It needs to be more widely appreciated that such support is needed for children whose first language or dialect is not standard English, for example children of West Indian origin. It is also vital to recognise that regard to children's first language and culture within the school curriculum is likely to benefit their learning of English as a second language.

Mother tongue and bilingual education

Britain lags behind other Western European countries in its provision for the teaching of mother tongue, and for teaching through the medium of mother tongue, which is bilingual education. According to the Government Survey in response to the 1977 EC Directive, 12 per cent of the 375,000 British children from homes where English is not the first language were receiving mother-tongue tuition. Only about two per cent of this was in maintained schools, with the rest being provided in the form of voluntary classes by the minority communities themselves. In France and the Netherlands about a third of foreign children are estimated to be receiving tuition in their language and culture of origin, with the proportion rather lower in Belgium.

There is limited relevance to Britain in much of the mother-tongue teaching provided in these countries. As it was set up to aid the re-integration of foreign children into their country of origin, the courses and methods used by foreign teachers, who are in some cases employed by foreign governments, are usually unrelated to the normal curriculum. Lessons are often provided outside the school timetable, and have no more influence on normal schooling than the community language classes run by ethnic minority groups in Britain. However, the 1977 EC Directive now requires the promotion of mother-tongue teaching in coordination with normal education, and there are some noteworthy examples of the integration of mother-tongue teaching into the normal curriculum in several EC countries. These appear to have educational and cultural benefits for the foreign children and also contribute to the intercultural education of indigenous children. It is Sweden, however, which offers the best example of commitment to mother-tongue and bilingual education. Although the Bullock Report (*A Language for Life, 1975*) and the report of the Swedish Immigration Commission (1974) both supported the case for the use of mother tongue within the school system, the response in Britain has been cautious, and developments small scale, whereas Sweden has during the past decade made active bilingualism the major plank of its education policy for minorities. Two-thirds of the eligible children of school age take up the right conferred in the 1977 Home Language Reform to teaching in the first language within normal school. This may be provided through withdrawal from normal classes for the teaching of mother tongue, or in the form of bilingual teaching, where the mother tongue is used as the medium of instruction, either for study guidance in various subjects or in the full-time home language classes.

The mother-tongue debate in this country has focused almost exclusively on mother-tongue rather than bilingual teaching, mainly in the form of the inclusion of Asian languages in the modern languages curriculum of secondary schools. However, a growing body of evidence has built up, not only from abroad but from projects in this country supported by the DES (particularly Mother-Tongue and English Teaching for Young Asian Children in Bradford, 1978–81, and the Linguistic Minorities Project, 1979–83) and by the EC (Bedford Mother Tongue Project, 1976–80, and the Schools Council Mother Tongue Project, 1981–84), to demonstrate that bilingual as well as mother-tongue teaching has a valuable role to play in schools. The principal benefits are in helping the transition to school of children whose first language is not English, continuing their conceptual development while competence in English is established, improving their emotional development, maintaining their cultural links, enabling them to add literacy to oral skills and to benefit from their bilingualism by further study in the secondary modern languages curriculum, allowing English-speaking pupils access to other than European languages, and contributing towards intercultural education.

The development of mother-tongue and bilingual education in Britain will require unequivocal official acceptance of the view that linguistic diversity is a national resource rather than a liability. That implies active DES encouragement to local education authorities to expand their curriculum provision in this area and to seek ways of increasing their support for voluntary language classes organised by the ethnic minority communities, with a view to coordinating the education which they provide with mainstream schooling.

An increase in the supply of bilingual teachers would be a prerequisite of any significant development of mother-tongue teaching in schools. National action in support of special access courses leading to teacher training for educated bilingual people with teaching potential would be necessary, while the employment of instructors could be justified as an interim measure in some situations, particularly in the transition to school. In the long run, teacher supply for mother tongue and bilingual education in maintained schools will depend on the degree to which bilingual children are themselves educated to appropriate levels of attainment in their first language and whether they enter teaching in sufficient numbers.

Staffing needs

The case for encouraging among ethnic minority children a higher participation rate in teaching rests not only on the need for bilingual teachers but on the importance of increasing the proportion of staff from ethnic minorities working in the education service at all levels if the aims of intercultural education are to be achieved. The example of successful foreign and ethnic minority teachers in some of the countries that I visited demonstrated that teachers who share with ethnic minority pupils the experience of more than one culture can give considerable impetus to intercultural education through their relationships with other staff and with pupils, and through their influence on the professional life of the school. In my view, it is vital for the future health of the education service in our multicultural society that it should attract a proportionate share of recruits from the British ethnic minorities and that debate should begin on how this goal can be achieved.

Acknowledgements

I am grateful to the AEC Trust and also to Derbyshire County Council and my colleagues there for making my study tour possible. I would like to thank all those who helped me, especially the following:

Britain

John Evans, Peter Broster (Derbyshire County Council), John Banks and John Singh (DES), Janet May (Education Management Information Exchange), Xavier Couillaud (Linguistic Minorities Project), Professor James Lynch (Sunderland Polytechnic), Dr Frank Molyneux (University of Nottingham).

France

Michelle Huart (Ministry of Education, Paris), Ferdnand Pau (Primary Inspector, Marseille), Francis Orsini and the staff of the Marseille CEFISEM, Jo Martinez and the staff of the Grenoble CEFISEM.

West Germany

Dr Christian Petry and the staff of the Regionale Arbeitstellen zur Förderung ausländischer Kinder and Jugendlicher (RAA), H-J Dumrese (Education Ministry, Bonn), H Hermann, Fr S Holzmann (Standing Conference of Ministers of Culture of the Federal States), E Woitschnik (Ministry of Culture, Baden-Würtemburg), E Jancke, G Weil (Berlin), K-H Walther, Fr Leckerbusch (North Rhine-Westphalia), E Barth (Schools Inspector, Osnabruck), C Kodron (German Institute for International Research in Education, Frankfurt), Fr I Gogolin (University of Essen).

Netherlands

L van der Gaag, F de Rijcke, L Elting, B Salverda (Ministry of Education and Science, The Hague), F Jacobs (Enschede Education Centre), G Meelker, S Drijver, H Klein (municipality of Dordrecht), Mrs G Felix-Timmermans, Amsterdam; Mr L Winnenhoff, Rotterdam; Mrs N van Doorn, State Inspector, Leiden.

Belgium

M Leurin, Schools Inspector (French Ministry of Education, Brussels), Mrs M-C Rosiers, Mrs L Pareyns, Provincial Service for the Reception of Immigrant Workers, Hasselt.

Sweden

Ms Monica Fägerborn, Mrs C Reimers (The Swedish Institute), Bertil Jakobsson (Commission on Migrants' Languages and Cultures in School and Adult Education), R Bergentoft (National Board of Education), O Norberg (municipality of Södertälje); Mrs K Thoren (Haninge); Mrs T Rosengren, Mrs B Bengtsson (Gothenburg); Mrs Britt-Inger Stockfeldt-Hoatson (National Immigration and Naturalisation Board), G Tingbjörn (SPRINS Project, University of Gothenburg), C-A Sparrman (University of Stockholm, School of Education).

Commission of the European Communities: L Jacoby.

Council of Europe: Mlle M Rolandi Ricci, Mlle A Trusso.